The Oldest Ranch in Texas

Rancho de la Purísima Concepción
A Ranch on the Road to History

Joe Wreford Hipp

EAKIN PRESS ✦ Fort Worth, Texas
www.EakinPress.com

Contents

"One generation passes away, and another generation comes: but the earth (the land) abides forever."
Ecclesiastes 1:4 (kjv paraphrased)

Generations of the Joseph Antonio Pérez Family

(Descendants will be shown next, the succeeding generation.)

Joseph Antonio Pérez (b. ca 1712) m. Paula Granado
1. Santiago Domingo*
2. Francisco Xavier
3. Joseph Guillermo
4. Clara
5. Juan Antonio
6. Juan Ignacio
7. Juan Francisco
8. Juan Joseph

Santiago Domingo (b. ca 1740) m. Maria Concepción de Carvajal
1. Juan Ignacio *
2. Maria Francisca de los Dolores
3. Maria Barbara
4. Manuel Salvador
5. Joseph Manuel
6. Joseph Maria
7. Maria Trinidad
8. Maria Ildefonsa Concepción
9. Jose Nicolas
10. Antonia Manuela Juana
11. Maria Telesfora
12. Juana Maria
13. Manuel Ignacio

Juan Ignacio Pérez (b. 1761) m. Clemencia Hernandez
1. Jose Ignacio *
2. Gertrudis

3. Concepción
4. Jose Antonio (adopted)

Jose Ignacio Pérez (b. 1786) m. Maria Josefa Cortinas
1. Ignacio
2. Jesus
3. Maria Trinidad
4. Maria Josefa de Jesus Anastacia Toribia *
5. Ignacio (the younger)
6. Concepción

Maria Josefa Pérez (b. April 26, 1824) m. Jacob Linn
1. Maria Isabel de la Trinidad
2. Casimira de la Concepción *

Casimira de la Concepción (Pérez) Linn (b. March 4, 1868) m. Frank T. Walsh
1. Mary
2. Anita
3. Lottie
4. Bessie
5. Frank T. Jr
6. Harry J.
7. Edward P. *

Edward P. Walsh (b. 1908) m. Mary Louise Yarborough
1. Caroline
2. Patricia *

Patricia Concepción Walsh (b. 1946) m. John Hart Small
1. John Edward
2. Patrick
3. Elizabeth

List of Illustrations

Preface

My first introduction to South Texas ranching was the summer of 1953, as a newspaper intern on the *San Antonio Express-News*. The late R. G. Jordan, farm and ranch editor, took his two week vacation while I was there and the managing editor, Bill Bellamy, sent me (his Texas Aggie) to the stockyards to occupy Mr. Jordan's office and write his Cattle Clatter column. That began my education about ranching in South Texas, walking the catwalks above the stock pens and talking to anyone who would give me the time.

Forty years and two careers later I found a story that would have made my stay at the stockyards more interesting, a story about the oldest family-owned ranch in Texas, occupied and operated by descendants of the original grantee. I first got the idea of writing a story about the oldest ranch in Texas over a decade ago. The oldest of anything deserves proper recognition. Other writing projects took precedence and I wasn't sure I knew which ranch was truly the oldest.

In the meantime, I read a number of books about ranching and absorbed as much as I could of Jack Jackson's huge work, *Los Mestenos*. I talked with Judge Robert Thonhoff at a meeting in Victoria and wasn't sure I was on the right track to resolve the question.

I'm not a historian and I'm not a rancher. I'm a journalist with an interest in the past. What I found convinced me Rancho de la Purísima Concepción was the oldest ranch in Texas, and perhaps North America.[1] It has been owned and operated by the same family for more than 200 years and is nestled between Leon Creek and the Medina River south of San Antonio, Texas. Only nine miles south of the Alamo, as the crow flies, the ranch seems out of place on the fringe of an urban area now ranked seventh largest in the United States. In San Antonio, where fiestas and celebrations are commonplace for the significant and mundane, there was no celebrating in River City (a San Antonio pseudonym) when Rancho de la Purísima Concepción turned 200 years old. How it has survived, and if it will survive the next few years, is my story.

Ask history-challenged Texans to name the oldest ranch in the state and the usual response is—"King Ranch." The King Ranch, founded in 1853, is arguably the most famous and among the largest. But, it's not the oldest by a long shot. The earliest recorded Spanish grant of private ranch land in Texas (not Nuevo Santander or later Tamaulipas) was to the Andres Hernandez family. That ranch was established in the 1750s. The Flores family established a ranch on the Cibolo in the same period. Those earliest family-owned ranches have long since been sold.

Grants made by Spain in Nuevo Santander north of the Rio Grande must be considered in any determination because they are now part of Texas. Las Noriecitas Ranch in Jim Hogg County could be the oldest recorded grant between the Nueces and the Rio Grande rivers. It is listed in the Texas Land Heritage Program as dating back to 1740. However, the Texas General Land Office publication, "Guide to Spanish and Mexican Land Grants in South Texas," challenges that claim by stating in its introduction that private ownership "between the Nueces and Rio Grande rivers, with the exception of the Jose Vazquez Borrego grant, dates from 1767." It acknowledges that requests for individual land allocations were on file as early as 1753, "but administrative and bureaucratic delays postponed distribution for over a decade." That same document shows the Noriecitas ranch as being granted by

Mexico in 1835. Such disconnects were common as I searched for answers.

There are other family-owned ranches dating back to the 1700s, and listed in the Texas Land Heritage Program. However, as in the case of the Noriecitas ranch, there is conflicting information. Documentation is hard to find and much of it is in the hands of the owners, which leads me back to Rancho de la Purísima Concepción.

The original grantee, Don Juan Ignacio Pérez de Casanova, was listed in 1795 among those "legitimately engaged in the business of raising cattle."[2] As early as 1793 he was given a license to round up "unbranded bulls and export cattle from Texas."[3] This type of license was usually reserved for those who owned *ranchos*. Noted ranch historian Jack Jackson suggests the Pérez family could have been ranching on the Medina as far back as 1780. This is quite likely considering arrangements made between mission padres and the Spanish settlers for "use" of mission lands. The Pérez presence on the Medina would have provided a protective buffer against marauding Indians on the road to "El Atascoso," an outlying ranch managed by San Jose Mission Indians. Successive family members have changed the name, known in subsequent years as the Stone Rancho, Pérez Ranch, Linn Ranch, Rancho de Leon, and Walsh Ranch. However, the ranch was originally named by Pérez in honor of the mission Nuestra Señora de la Purísima Concepción.

Parts of the original grant have been sold outside the family, and an adjacent 16,000 acres granted Pérez in 1808 was settled and claimed by new Texans after Santa Anna was defeated in 1836. A landmark suit filed with the Texas Supreme Court and recorded in the Texas General Land Office[4] maintained that the original grant of a league of land westward from the confluence of Leon Creek and the Medina River belonged to the Pérez family.

Indians and Spanish armies crossed the ranch as Nueva España's state of Texas struggled to survive. Indian tribes hunted game and foraged for nuts along the Medina and "one-eyed" General Arredondo, after the Battle of Medina in 1813, pursued the surviving members of the revolutionary army across the ranch and into San Antonio. To compare Michener's fictional Rancho El Codo in his novel Texas to Rancho de la Purísima Concepción would be a disservice to the truth. But, the similarities are striking and reconfirm the adage "truth can be stranger than fiction." In recent years the ranch became a pawn in yet another power struggle.

To tell the story in an appealing form for a large audience, license has been taken with some historical references. Hopefully this will not distract academic historians and will provide an arresting tale for readers of all ages and disciplines.

Acknowledgments

This story can only be told because a family of Texas ranchers made it happen. The current generations of that family, more specifically the family of Patricia and John Small, are dedicated to continuing their heritage of operating a family-owned ranch. Their help with interviews, photographs, access to the ranch, editing drafts for accuracy of family history, and the firsthand knowledge of historic locations, made this book possible. The next generation, John Edward, Patrick, and Elizabeth Small, are just as dedicated to the ranching tradition and will make it survive if at all possible. Thanks for your help and sharing your story.

A writer without access to a reader can be likened to a rancher without access to water; the potential for failure is always there. Thank you, Kay Cavanaugh, for repeated readings of the manuscript. Kay is an educator, principal of Fernandez Elementary School in San Antonio's Northside School District, an avid reader, and a lady with firsthand ranching experience.

And, finally, to the folks in the nonfiction work group at San Antonio Writer's Guild, thanks for your comments on the first efforts to write this story.

Chapter One

Vamos allá!

The beginning of this story reaches back in time and place to a stone *casa* near Laguna of Tenerife in the Canary Islands. Phelipe and Joseph Antonio, likeable and robust teenaged sons of Domingo and Maria Peres (Pérez) de Casanova, packed their belongings into a sail-canvas bag. Adding last minute items from the kitchen, hard-crusted rolls and cheese, the brothers joked nervously about leaving home. The year was 1729, and the Spanish galleon, *Dos Amigos* (two friends), was docked in Santa Cruz de Tenerife harbor taking on water and supplies. Arriving at Tenerife, the captain announced he was looking for additional crew members for the voyage to Nueva España. Phelipe and Joseph Antonio signed on as members of the crew.

Among their last chores that July morning was opening the spillway gate of the *acequia* and allowing water to flood the family garden. The gate had been closed, their bag packed, and sad-faced Domingo and Maria waited in an ox-drawn two-wheeled cart to take their sons to the harbor. Their decision allowing Phelipe and Joseph to sail aboard the *Dos Amigos* was not difficult. Other family members had sailed from the Canary Islands to the new world, some landing in Santo Domingo and settling that Spanish possession. Their great-uncle, Francisco Terreros, had settled near Jalapa in Nueva España's province of Veracruz.

Another respected (however distant) relative, the

1

eighteenth century Marques de San Miguel de Aguayo, was appointed governor of Coahuila and Texas in 1719. Traveling through Nueva España, he established *presidios* at Adaes and Bahia[5] to fend off venturesome Frenchmen intent on settling land claimed by Spain. The Marques reported to King Carlos in the 1720s that only the settlement of families in the new territory would insure Spain's hold on the land. The king initially agreed to send 100 families from the Canary Islands to Nueva España. That immigration would begin in 1730.

Phelipe and Joseph were restless and adventurous, with an enormous sense of family. Neither could read nor write, but they had grown up listening to tales of noble ancestors and exploits of living relatives. Despite their lack of education, they yearned for more in life than a plot of land on a volcanic rocky slope, tending goats and a garden. Making a surprise visit to Uncle Francisco Terreros' *rancho* near Jalapa was an opportunity they could not pass.

The cart rumbled along the worn roadway (once used by aboriginal Guanches to herd goats about the island) while the boisterous brothers walked alongside, talking loudly and gesturing excitedly about the adventure lying ahead. Their parents sat quietly in the cart, watching and listening, fearing these were the last words they would hear from Joseph and Phelipe.

Reaching the dock, Maria was helped from the cart. She embraced her sons with tears in her eyes and quietly spoke, "Mis hijos, 'Más vale buen nombre que muchas riquezas, y mejor es favor que plata y oro'." ("My sons, 'More valuable is a good name than much wealth, and more favored than silver and gold'." Proverbs 22:1.) For her it was indeed a solemn occasion, a moment in time to savor and prolong despite the eagerness of her sons to be on their way. Domingo turned the ox for their trip back to Laguna, and Maria kissed the boys farewell. It was the last time Domingo and Maria would see their sons.

Joseph and Phelipe joined two experienced sailing friends from Tenerife as shipmates on the *Dos Amigos*,

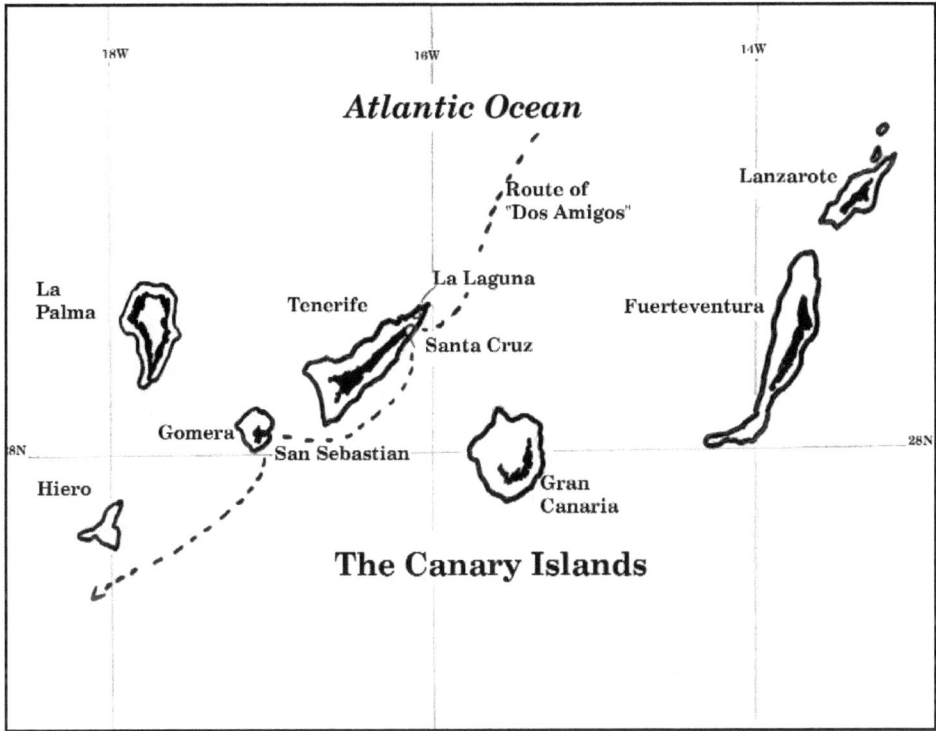

18W   16W   14W

Atlantic Ocean

Route of
"Dos Amigos"

Lanzarote

La Laguna

La
Palma

Tenerife

Fuerteventura

Santa Cruz

Gomera

San Sebastian

28N

8N

Gran
Canaria

Hiero

The Canary Islands

*Map of Canary Islands showing route of
Dos Amigos.*

Francisco Arocha and Vicente Travieso. The ship sailed the next day with the morning tide and by midday Pico de Teide, the ancient volcano, was all they could see of Tenerife as the ship moved along swiftly, benefitting from strong trade winds off the coast of North Africa. Their southwesterly course took them to San Sebastian on the island of Gomera, where the *Dos Amigos* made a final call for crew members and supplies. "At San Sebastian in Gomera, while the crew was filling the water casks and bringing aboard a fresh supply of meat for the voyage, the captain hired two young fishermen, Ignacio de Armas, twenty-one years old, and his brother Martin, nineteen, natives of Gomera."[6] During the voyage, the six young

Canary Islanders became fast friends, little knowing how closely their futures would be linked.

The *Dos Amigos* was blown westward by a series of squall lines and the young Canary Islanders earned their passage hoisting and lowering sails on the wave-swept decks. In twenty-eight days they reached Havana, Cuba. The de Armas brothers had been at sea long enough and went ashore to seek their fortune.

Continuing to Veracruz with its cargo from Cadiz, and the four young men from Tenerife, the *Dos Amigos* arrived in the Bay of Campeche on a steamy August morning and was moored in the port by late afternoon. The Pérez brothers collected their belongings and found a caravan going north to Jalapa via Cerro Gordo, a lush green mountain pass. Reaching Jalapa, they were directed to the *rancho* of their Uncle Francisco and marveled at the vastness and verdant richness of his land. So began their life in Nueva España.

Arocha and Travieso joined a pack train traveling west toward Mexico City. Stopping at Cholula, the sailors found work as herdsmen on a nearby *rancho*.

Summer of 1730

The year passed quickly for the Pérez brothers. Working for their great-uncle was an education in ranching. First they had learned to care for horses, then to ride them. Their teachers were the *vaqueros* who maintained the herds of horses and cattle. One day on the *rancho* of Francisco Terreros, a representative of the government arrived looking for animals to purchase. Francisco Duval, the king's agent, was purchasing a remuda of horses to carry Canary Island settlers from Veracruz to San Antonio de Bejar.[7] He found the best horses for the least money at Terreros' *rancho*, a business trait continuing in later generations of the Pérez family.

On hearing Duval's story about the Canary Islanders, the restless Phelipe (Felipe) and Joseph Antonio (Jose) asked Duval and their uncle if they could join the settlers. Duval allowed them to accompany him back to Veracruz where the settlers would determine their fate. Great-uncle Francisco gave each youth two fine horses to begin their journey.

Presenting themselves in Veracruz, they were surprised to learn the de Armas brothers, last seen in Havana, had also joined the group. Felipe and Jose Pérez were readily accepted by the settlers as worthy participants in the king's colonization attempt and proceeded with them from Veracruz to Cuautitlan. It was August 1730. The journey began in hot, humid weather. As they penetrated the mountains southeast of Mexico City, temperatures dropped unexpectedly to near freezing and flurries of snow whirled around them. Even the Pérez brothers, who had wintered in Jalapa riding the high ranges and sleeping outdoors, were unprepared for the weather change.

After a careful descent from the mountains, Duval led the settlers east of Mexico City to avoid the confusion, danger, and cost of moving cattle through congested city streets. It also reduced the chance of losing his naive charges to temptations of the thriving metropolis. Arriving in Cuautitlan during late August, they had taken nearly a month to cover the difficult 300 miles, a trip now accomplished in a matter of hours on a super highway. Welcoming services were held for the settlers in the beautiful church of the Franciscan convent of Cuautitlan. The *alcalde* rented three large buildings to accommodate the settlers during their stay in Cuautitlan. The travelers had never seen a more opulent church and were impressed by the attention they received.

Meanwhile, Arocha and Travieso, the sailors turned goat herdsmen, heard about the Canary Island settlers traveling to the land the king had promised them. Collecting their meager wages from the rancher, they hastened to join the settlers. Looking first in Mexico City, the young men were overwhelmed by the teeming population, the size of the buildings, and the numbers of car-

Carte du Mexique et de la Floride. 1703. Guillaume Delisle.
Overlaid with route of Dos Amigos and route of pobladores
from Veracruz to San Antonio de Bexar.

riages careening through the streets. After several
queries they were directed to Cuautitlan and reunited
with their sailing companions, and some old friends, the
Curbelo family from Lanzarote.[8]

At a hastily prepared fiesta in honor of the renewed
acquaintance between Maria Ana Curbelo and Travieso,
and Juana Curbelo and Arocha, the *alcalde* reminded the
group only heads of families could receive land and hold
office in San Antonio de Bejar. Encouraged by the promise of full privileges as heads of households, and with the
viceroy's approval, Travieso and Arocha received permission to marry the Curbelo daughters. The weddings
spurred other romantic interests between single men and
women of the party, and before leaving Cuautitlan for

Saltillo a total of five marriages occurred. The de Armas and Pérez brothers observed the proceedings, but remained wary bachelors.

Having spent more than two months being treated royally in Cuautitlan, the settlers perhaps expected the royal treatment to continue in subsequent stops. With a fresh remuda of horses and mules, it was time for Francisco Duval to lead the Islanders from Cuautitlan November 15, 1730, on perhaps the most difficult and dangerous portion of their journey. For the newlyweds, this was a honeymoon trip to remember. They reached Saltillo December 11, by way of Queretaro and San Luis Potosi. In twenty-six days, the Islanders had covered more than 500 miles, over mountain trails rising to 8,000 feet, desert terrain without settlements to provide protection, and through bitter cold. Their military escort had protected them from *bandidos* (bandits) who customarily waylaid travelers on this section of the road to the *frontera* (frontier). The stress of the journey was beginning to tell on the older members of the party, and the Pérez brothers were glad they had only themselves to look after.

Saltillo was the last major Spanish settlement the Canary Island settlers would see on their journey to San Antonio de Bejar, and the royal treatment had diminished. Housing for the Canary Islanders in Saltillo was minimal to nonexistent. However, all the supplies promised for establishing their community in *Nueva España* had been assembled there; oxen, horses, mules, wooden yokes, ploughshares, axes, and other tools for sixteen families. The Pérez and de Armas brothers were considered as a family unit in the allocation of equipment.

Duval had his charges moving toward San Antonio de Bejar, January 28, 1731, with a fresh escort of soldiers. If an encounter with Indians were to occur, Duval expected it on this lonely stretch of land, where small herds of buffalo (bison) could still be seen. Resting in Monclova for two days, they continued northeastward, fording the frigid water of the Rio Sabinas (Salado) near present day Sabinas after three days of travel. It would be four more years before the Spanish founded the Presidio at Santa Rosa del Sacramento (now Melchor Muzquiz). A range of mountains appeared to block their route, but Duval had been this way before. Leading them through a pass and onto the flood plain of the Rio Grande, the Islanders were nearing El Presidio de San Juan Bautista, where Diego Ramon had received the Frenchman, Chevalier Louis Juchereau de St. Denis in 1714. It was the unexpected arrival of St. Denis at San Juan Bautista that precipitated the rush to colonize Texas with Spaniards.

As they approached this last outpost, the settlers were treated to a memorable sight. Following a winter pasture trail along the Rio Grande was a huge herd of bison, coated with frost on a cold, damp February morning. The great, shaggy beasts took little note of the band of travelers, only snorting and shaking their massive heads occasionally. Winter range for the bison herd extended as far south in Texas as present day Laredo. In Mexico they were frequently seen near Saltillo. For perhaps an hour they watched the herd move northward then circled behind the bison to reach El Presidio de San Juan Bautista while there was still light in the overcast sky.

The unpredictable rise and fall of the Rio Grande had impacted the plans of armies and expeditions for at least two centuries. Not to be delayed, the settlers forded the river the next morning using Francia (Frenchman's) Crossing and camped three days on the east bank, opposite the presidio, while preparations were made for the last leg of their journey. Departing February 27, they followed the Lower Presidio Road (as it became known later) and reached the tree-shaded Medina River, March 7. There Duval had them rest and prepare for a final day of travel into San Antonio de Bejar.

Until this time they had seen few Indians, and those appeared friendly. No doubt the soldiers accompanying the Canary Islanders made hostile approach a risky proposition. But, a band of Apaches had been seen on the Medina not far from where the settlers were now camping. Before dawn a stealthy group of Indians stole into the camp and rustled many of the settlers' horses while the weary soldiers slept at their posts. The Indians and horses were gone before the soldiers could mount a defense. No lives were lost, but an angry Duval gave the soldiers a verbal shellacking for their carelessness and sent several immediately to track the Indians. He dispatched a lone horseman to Presidio San Antonio de Bejar for help. The raid upset Duval's plans and prolonged by a day their stay on the Medina.

While waiting for additional soldiers and horses to arrive from the fort, Felipe and Jose Pérez received permission from Duval to explore the land north of the Medina. There was very little brush on the open, rolling prairie and the young men could smell the fresh, pungent evidence that wild cattle and bison roamed the land.

Early on the morning of March 9, the settlers mounted their horses and, accompanied by reinforcements from the *Presidio*, their cattle, and other trappings, rode toward San Antonio. As history records it, they appeared at the gate of the presidio at 11:00 A.M., give or take a few minutes. After a journey of nearly a year from the Canary Islands, the Spanish settlers/*pobladores* had arrived!

Chapter Two

1777–1808
Founding of the Ranch

$\mathcal{T}$he first years Felipe and Jose Antonio spent in Nueva España were very different from what they had imagined. Instead of being treated as the first step of nobility (*hidalgos* or *dons*, a title granted them by the king of Spain), they had to scratch out their own living on the share of land received by Felipe, the elder. It was humbling for a *"don"* to plant and protect his crops, build a house, cook meals, and perform menial civic duties. The quality of meals available to the bachelor brothers brought Jose to realize marriage might be more than a convenience, perhaps a necessity.

In time Jose chose a bride, the dark-haired and beautiful Paula Granado, daughter of Maria Robiana de Bethencourt and Juan Rodriguez Granado. Jose and Paula had eight children: Santiago Domingo, 1740; Francisco Xavier, 1746; Joseph Guillermo, 1747; Clara, 1751; Juan Antonio, 1753; Juan Ignacio, 1756; Juan Francisco, 1758; and Juan Joseph, 1759.[9] His mother-in-law, widowed during the journey to Nueva España, was the "social leader" of the Canary Islanders' community. Shortly after arriving in San Antonio de Bejar she received a large inheritance and married a young Canary Islander, Jose Antonio's friend from the *Dos Amigos,* Martin Lorenzo de Armas.

Remoteness and difficulties with Comanches and Lipan Apaches discouraged early settlers from purchasing land on the Medina, but Jose Antonio had his eye on the expanse of land between the Leon and the Medina. Jose's oldest son, Domingo, entered the Spanish militia in 1756 and married Maria Concepción de Carvajal a few years later. The prolific couple had thirteen children. Their first son, born in 1761, was named Juan Ignacio and baptized on July 16 of that year.

With Domingo in the militia, Jose considered it safe to take his family on armed outings to the San Jose Mission pastures near the river. Tolerating her son-in-law's adventurous spirit, Maria Robiana would occasionally venture to the Medina River on his outings when her health and social calendar allowed. With muskets at the ready, and safety in numbers, the Pérez de Casanova clan enjoyed the outings. Although mission cattle could be found on the Medina, herdsmen from the mission seldom ventured beyond the Leon to round up cattle because of the danger from Indian rustlers. *El despoblado* was an unforgiving enemy if entered without caution.

It was the year 1777, and colonists in New England were still in the process of signing a Declaration of Independence. East Texas colonists led by Gil Ybarbo had been moved out of Bexar by Governor Juan Maria, Baron de Ripperda, and resettled in Villa de Bucareli on the Trinity River. Antonio Maria de Bucareli was the viceroy of New Spain, and El Fuerte del Cibolo,[10] garrisoned with twenty Spanish soldiers, provided some protection for *ranchos* between San Antonio and La Bahia. Work on the Upper Labor Ditch in San Antonio was in progress. Jose Pérez had only recently been absolved of any wrongdoing in a case of alleged land fraud. His mother-in-law testified in his behalf, along with other members of the Canary Island settlers. Frederick Chabot, in his book about early San Antonio, recorded the event involved lands ". . . acquired from the *Cabrera*." If he meant *Cabildo,* it would be more easily understood. Quite likely it had to do with the governor's inquiry concerning cattle roundups and on whose land the roundups were being accomplished. A footnote to the events of the year was Domingo Pérez' appointment to sergeant in the militia.

To celebrate his victory in court, Jose planned a fiesta on the Medina River that fall. Not only were they celebrating Jose's successful defense, rumors persisted of a great cattle drive being organized by the government. The governor of Louisiana had asked for 2,000 head of longhorn cattle to feed his army and if the rumor were true, cattle prices would rise throughout the province. Although Mission San Jose claimed the land, it acquiesced to Jose Antonio Pérez de Casanova's entrpreneurial cattle raising presence on the land as beneficial to the community.

While the women prepared food, Jose held court with his friends on a log by the quiet flowing river. Sergeant Domingo Pérez was on duty at the presidio. Domingo's wife and children were present, including their oldest son, Juan Ignacio.

From his childhood, Juan Ignacio Pérez de Casanova had visited the land between the Medina River and Leon Creek, exploring the *arroyos,* gathering pecans from trees that grew in the river bottom, and playing with Indian friends from the Espada Mission. Grandfather Jose (Joseph Antonio) Pérez had coveted this land from the time he first laid eyes on it and would take his family there on every occasion.

Juan Ignacio, his brothers, sisters, and cousins, were taking advantage of the warm day to play along the Medina. Sixteen-year-old Juan Ignacio was an accomplished horseback rider, a skill learned from his grandfather and Indian friends as he grew up. Bareback, or in the ornate saddle purchased for him in Saltillo, Juan Ignacio could ride and rope with the best in Bexar. His accuracy with a musket was seldom challenged, as most skills were challenged in those days. He learned the native tongues of the mission Indians, and the Lipan Apache. Sign language common to other tribes had been easy for him to master. Strangers passing through Villa San Fernando were often greeted by this gregarious and curious young Spaniard.

Status in the community and family ties allowed the Pérez boys to attend Christoval de los Santos Coy's school. Maria Curbelo de los Santos Coy, wife of the schoolmaster and one of the original Canary Island travelers to New Spain, insisted all of their descendants would learn to read and write. In her later years Maria was affectionately called *"tia Canaria"* (Aunt Canary) and outlived all other original settlers. Most of the Canary Island settlers could neither read nor write, a severe obstacle for leadership of a community. The most aggressive student in the third generation of the Pérez settlers was Juan Ignacio. As Bexar archives would later reveal, Juan Ignacio was a profuse, legible writer, and keeper of detailed records.

An extended drought had reduced the river flow and there were many places where one could easily wade across the river boundary into the province of Coahuila. While the smaller children launched strips of bark into the slow-moving stream from a graveled beach, Juan Ignacio galloped his horse beneath the towering pecan trees and whooped like an Indian. One day this would be his land. He knew it.

Winter of 1794–1795

A scant hundred yards east of the Camino Real crossing of the Medina River (now known as the Pérez Crossing, or the low-water crossing on Applewhite Road) a campfire glowed beneath giant native pecan trees on the shallow north bank of the river. Darkness settled above the canopy of pecan trees and a bright-white moon appeared to drift slowly westward, forming a lattice work of shadows on the small clearing by the campfire. In the thick underbrush a cougar howled as feral hogs and javelina foraged beyond the circle of light. On ridges north and south of the campfire, coyotes yipped and wailed.

By the campfire, rosy-cheeked Clemencia Hernandez, wife of Juan Ignacio Pérez, stirred a pot of *sopa de ajo* to ward off the buffalo gnats, animals, evil spirits and anything else that does not like the smell of garlic. The daughter of Jose Placido Hernandez and Rosalia Montes de Oca, Clemencia was a fitting mate for the sturdy young officer of the Spanish Royalist Army assigned to the militia at San Antonio. Clemencia's father was among the first of several Hernandez descendants to receive a Royal Grant (recorded in the Spanish Archives, July 10, 1769).[11]

Juan Ignacio's education in the school of Santos Coy, along with family position in the community, had earned him a commission in the militia. Following secularization of the missions and a liberal policy of grants to officers of the militia, Juan Ignacio had the opportunity to claim the grant of his choice, a league of land (more than 4,000 acres) between the Medina River and Leon Creek.

The Pérez family had often visited the banks of the Medina River by horseback and wagon to enjoy the pristine beauty of the land and feast off wild game they could snare or shoot. They brought goats to barbecue if the hunting was poor, and roasted wild game if luck was with them. Occasionally they would slaughter a bison from the dwindling herds grazing near San Antonio in the late eighteenth century. All the variety of game in the area could be found on the league of land nestled between the Medina River and Leon Creek. Small wonder Juan Ignacio petitioned for this spot as his grant.

Clemencia saw the flickering torches as Juan Ignacio, his brothers, and cousins made their way down from the work site to the shelter of the pecan grove, and began immediately to ladle garlic soup over chunks of hard bread placed in the bottom of large earthen bowls. When her chickens were producing eggs, she would crack an egg into each bowl of the hot soup. But the hot summer had continued into the fall, and her hens were still not producing eggs. With a strong, shrill voice, she called for her children, ten-year-old Jose Ignacio, and dark-haired Gertrudis, to bring their toddling baby sister, Concepción, and sit by the campfire.

Their stone *casa,* modeled after homes in the Canary Islands, was slowly taking shape and another day of work had ended. The house was being built on high ground with a cleared area of pasture land on three sides to warn of intruders. Less than fifty yards south the land dropped off into the Medina River bottoms. A bluff created by years of erosive flooding was precipitous and provided protection on that side. A well had been dug a few yards west of the house, yielding abundant water in a stratum of sand and gravel not far below the surface.

The night air soon resounded with human sounds, laughter and singing, and a guitar plucked tentatively by one of Clemencia's talented sisters. Rooting javelina grunted and moved away from the revelry, but the coyotes only yipped and wailed louder.

First Lieutenant Juan Ignacio Pérez appeared satisfied with the work on his house. He was following instructions given him by his grandfather, building a stone house like those found on Tenerife. The walls would withstand any assault, except that of a cannon, and provide cool shelter in the summer. His land also provided stones to fashion the walls. Many of the stones he gathered as a youth wandering the area with his Indian friends, piling the stones in cairns to signify a premature claim on the land, and to mark a stash of nuts from the bountiful pecan trees along the river bottom. The mission Indian boys from Espada and San Jose y San Miguel de Aguayo taught him to hunt, where to gather nuts, to speak their language, and introduced him to tribal customs, all of which contributed to his later success as a soldier and scout. Now he was the undisputed owner of the land. He had walked with the surveyor and performed the customs of claiming the land, throwing stones, pulling grass, and proclaiming himself owner in a loud voice.

An astute horse trader, but with an eye for fairness in all his dealings, Juan Ignacio had recently met a North American named Philip Nolan and was mixing his home building chores with the business of rounding up a herd of horses for Nolan to perhaps purchase. The horses on his ranch were wild, and corralling them in a narrow ravine leading to the Medina River was the method he used to gather Nolan's horses. It was a method the Indians had taught Juan Ignacio. The narrow ravine on

*One of several narrow ravines on the ranch
that lead to the river.*

his *rancho* was just below their campsite on the river. The horses had been captured earlier in the day and, as the family sang and ate their way into the evening, those same horses could be heard whinnying and stamping their hooves in the gravel bottom of the ravine. Nolan was due to arrive the next day to examine the horses. The going price for horses at that time in Texas was one to two pesos a head. The story of Philip Nolan is told in *Philip Nolan and Texas, Expeditions to the Unknown Land, 1791-1801,* by Maurine T. Wilson and Jack Jackson. They note that Nolan pastured his horses on the Medina while waiting to take them east.

Overhead the moon cast stark shadows over the river bottom. Two branch-covered *jacales* had been erected as sleeping quarters for the women and children. While Juan Ignacio pondered the next day's work, Clemencia put their children to bed. The men bedded down by the fire, wearied from another day of work.

Before spring came in 1795, Juan Ignacio's *ranchero* was livable, stables had been built, and a small herd of cattle rounded up and branded. Pedro Huizar, a carpenter and *alcalde* at Concepción, helped his friend in finishing the interior of the stone casa. After branding, the cattle were allowed to roam the *despoblado* safe from other Spaniards, but not from the Indians. Several mustangs had been herded into a makeshift corral where Juan Ignacio spent his evenings breaking them to ride. This was a good life for Lieutenant Pérez. His military duties, while demanding on occasion, allowed him to spend long periods with his family at the *rancho*. He also was gaining a reputation as an exporter of cattle from Texas and land buyer.

In 1795, Jose Ignacio bought a rock house ". . . situated in the district of the Plaza de Armas; its frontage is on the South where it is bounded by the Calle Real; its depth is eight varas on the north, where it is bounded by land and house of Joseph Manuel Jimenez; on the West by land of Mariano Menchaca and on the East by land and house of the said purchaser."[12] He paid 150 gold pesos for the property.

As a thirty-five-year-old lieutenant in the *compania volante,* Juan Ignacio frequently led patrols in pursuit of outlaws and renegade Indians, and was acclaimed by Governor Manuel Munoz as a scout and Indian fighter. Pérez knew the land and the Indians, and was at home on horseback. Andres Benito Courbier, a Frenchman in the service of the Spanish government, was interested in Juan Ignacio's knowledge of the Lipanes (Lipans), an eastern tribe of Apaches. Early records indicate a Lipan Apache village existed on the Colorado River near present-day Austin, Texas. Courbier recorded an incident in 1796 when Pérez was out with a work party near the banks of the San Marcos River. (See Appendix A) The Apaches stole several horses from the party in broad daylight and fled. Pérez quickly mounted his horse, secured horses for several of the work party and followed the raiding band of Apaches into their camp. In the exchange of gunfire (some Indians had already swapped their bows and arrows for captured muskets) Juan Ignacio was wounded in his right shoulder. Despite his wound, he recovered all but one horse and extracted a promise from the subdued Indians to replace the horse that could not be found.[13]

Living three leagues from the village had its drawbacks and often the family would stay at their home on the Calle Real while Juan Ignacio was on patrol or chasing Indians. The two- to three-hour ride on horseback from *Presidio de Bexar* to his ranch made each commuting day longer.

In 1804, after seven years of improvements on the ranch (including the start of a chapel), Pérez was promoted to captain and became commander of the San Antonio garrison of the Spanish militias and *presidiales*. Through the governor he exercised some authority over a famous regional cavalry unit known as the *compania volante* from San Carlos de Parras. They had been recently assigned to the old Valero mission compound as the historic presidio on Plaza de Armas was decommissioned and established east of the river. These men renamed the mission (turned presidio) the Alamo, after their hometown near Parras.[14]

Commander Pérez needed a *"commandancia"* (military commander's residence) in town with a view of the parade ground and barracks. Such accommodations did not come with the militia commander's job. Of the properties he had already acquired in Villa San Fernando, none suited his fancy as a proper *"commandancia."* However, Captain Pérez managed to buy a thick-walled adobe house on Plaza de Armas (Military Plaza, as it is known today) from Capt. Jose Menchaca for 800 pesos. It might be called a "distress" sale since Captain Menchaca was leaving town hurriedly. That it was sold as a private residence raises the question whether it had ever before been a *"commandancia"* for the presidio. Little did Pérez suspect this acquisition would eventually become part of San Antonio history. The date was May 17, 1804. To add historical perspective, three days earlier, May 14, 1804, Meriwether Lewis and William Clark left St. Louis on their exploration of the Louisiana Territory. The westward push by Anglo-Americans was beginning.

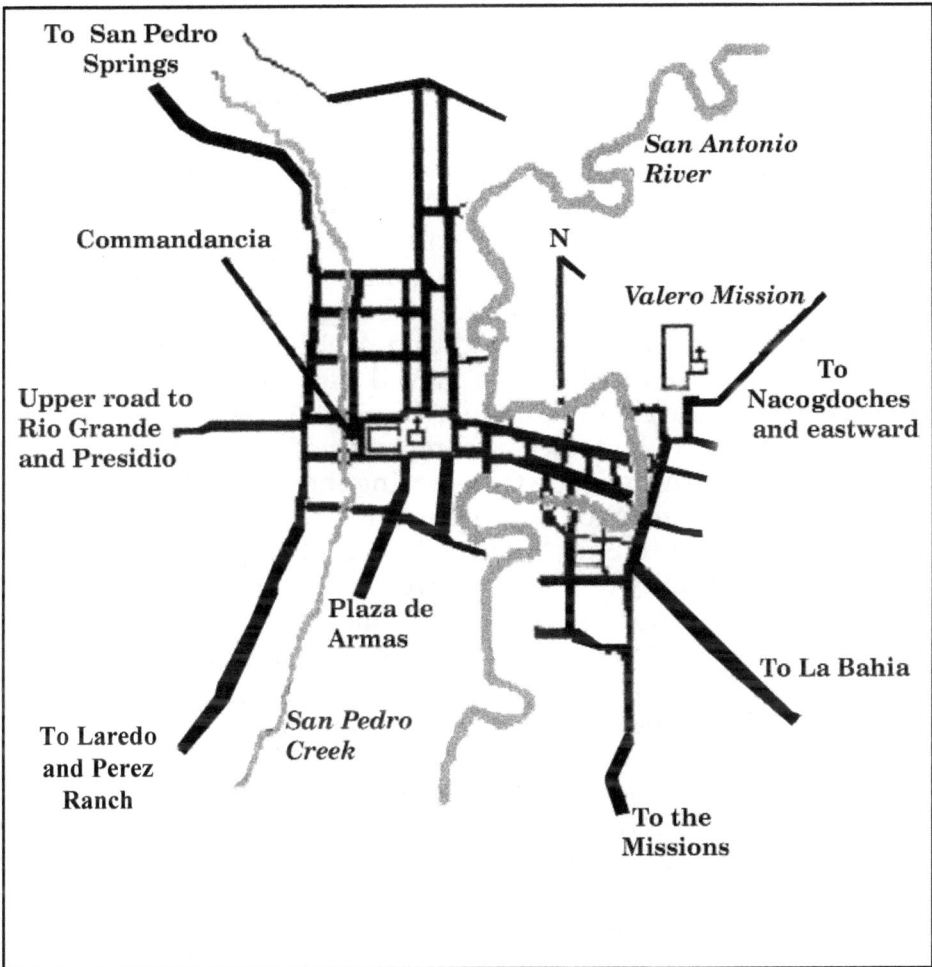

Downtown San Antonio 1804 showing location of
commandancia.

Juan Ignacio and Clemencia had a son and two daughters when they moved into town. The son, Jose Ignacio, preferred life on the ranch. Since he was a mature young man of eighteen years, Jose was allowed to stay in the stone house where he could look after the cattle and crops. Clemencia and Juan Ignacio adapted slowly to life in town, but their daughters, Gertrudis and Concepción, were quick to appreciate the new surroundings. Their school master, Jose Antonio Francisco Ruiz, had married Maria Josefa Hernandez that spring, the sister of Clemencia Pérez. The well-mannered, European-educated school master, called Francisco, would be closely linked to the Pérez family by more than marriage.

There they resided, entertaining and being entertained as life on the frontier of New Spain became more cosmopolitan. Into this politically loose, but socially correct, society came Manuel Antonio Cordero y Bustamante. Cordero looked, talked, and acted the part of a military man. He was respected and acclaimed by all who knew him. Colonel Cordero moved his governor's office from Montelovez in Coahuila to San Antonio. Shortly after his arrival he took two companies of troops and rode eastward to Nacogdoches reasserting the Crown's interest in the remote reaches of the province.

Returning to San Antonio, Governor Cordero accepted the hospitality of Captain Pérez, who graciously asked the new governor to share his formidable home on Military Plaza. The long, low frontage of his home on the plaza faced east and provided a shaded resting area for visitors during afternoon siestas. A promenade extended the length of the block facing the plaza. There were ten rooms in the home allowing some privacy, and a small loft at the rear overlooked the garden. The garden extended to the west ending at San Pedro Creek.

Cordero established himself as a vigorous leader in the community. His first priorities were construction of a bridge and avenue to cross the San Antonio River, and building a sanitary meat market. The avenue became present day Commerce Street and the sanitary meat market was located inside the horseshoe bend of the San Antonio River. Cordero later found the beauty of *doña* Gertrudis, the captain's seventeen-year-old daughter, a distraction which would eventually lead him to marriage.

Governor Cordero stayed in the Pérez home, had an office there, and received many official visitors in the house during his term of office. The house became known as the "Governor's Palace." It was there, in 1807, Cordero entertained the American explorer Zebulon Pike. Although Pike's description of San Antonio was "a town without a decent place to reside," he stated Governor Cordero was an excellent host. "Everything appeared to be in a flourishing and improving state, owing to the examples and encouragement given to industry, politeness and civilization by their excellent governor Cordero and his colleague Herrera: also the large body of troops maintained at that place in consequence of the difference existing between the United States and Spain," according to Pike's notes. "Don Antonio Cordero is about 5 ft. 10 in. in height, 50 years of age, fair complexion, and blue eyes; he wore his hair turned back, and in every part of his deportment was legibly written 'The Soldier'."[15]

Life was not idyllic, despite the order Cordero was bringing to San Antonio. There were still Indian raids, although none directed at Rancho de la Purísima Concepción. A former mission settlement called Las Cabras, about eight miles south-southeast of town, was attacked by a band of Lipan Apaches. A man from the mission rode into San Antonio to sound the alarm.

Gathering his *compania volante,* Pérez galloped to the rescue only to find the settlement in smoldering ruins when they arrived. As his soldiers fanned out to search for Indians and survivors, Pérez took one group of men up a small canyon near where the settlement's church once stood. He cautioned his men to not all fire at once if they saw Apaches. The Apaches could fire as many as fifteen arrows in the time it would take for a soldier to fire and reload his gun.[16]

From a distance Pérez saw what appeared to be a

body covered with weeds and grass on the canyon wall. He asked his men to dismount and investigate. They approached the area cautiously fearing Indians might still be around. Much to their surprise they found a statue of the Blessed Virgin smeared with war paint. The statue had been taken from the church and used by the Indians for target practice. Tips of arrows and marks left by spears disfigured the statue.

Carrying the statue back to San Antonio, Captain Pérez had it restored and placed in the family chapel at the Governor's Palace. The "Room of the Blessed Virgin," as the chapel was called, had a niche on the north wall where the hand-carved wooden statue was worshiped. He is reputed to have taken it with him on all subsequent expeditions, and the statue has since been passed down through succeeding generations of the family. It is now in the family chapel of the Walsh homestead on Applewhite Road and is said to be an excellent example of seventeenth century Spanish craftsmanship.

Throughout this period Pérez was active in the life of the community, serving as *alcalde* for two terms, publishing orders on the sale of meat, appointing commissioners of the different *barrios,* presiding in legal proceedings, and maintaining the municipal archives. He made his first of many official visits to Nacogdoches in 1808.

Chapter Three

An Additional Grant

𝕿 he most significant event for the Pérez family in 1808 was a grant of four additional leagues of land west of the Medina to graze their stock. All the customs of the time were observed, including the ritual of being led over the land by the surveyor. "He threw stones, pulled grass, and performed the other acts of true possession, and taking him by the hand, I led him over the denounced tract, and in a loud and understandable voice I gave him possession which he received quietly and peacefully," wrote *don* Manuel Barrera in the survey recorded in the Spanish Archives of Bexar County.

Boundaries of the grant stretched from the juncture of Leon Creek and the Medina River west four leagues (a league is about three statute miles) to a point known as San Simon. San Simon was further identified as the point where Atascosa Creek joined the river. The boundary then turned south one league to a point known as Rosales. Having established the western most boundary, the surveyor turned southeast four leagues to a point known as Hidden Hill. The final measurement was north one league to La Barranca on the Medina, the starting point. La Barranca and the Medina crossing of the Lower Presidio Road appear to coincide with present-day Cassin Crossing. Juan Ignacio's *rancho* included more than 20,000 acres stretching from the confluence of the Medina River and Leon Creek in the east to near present-day Somerset in the west.

San Antonio de Bexar Circa 1810

Headwaters
San Antonio
River

To Nacogdoches

San Pedro
Springs

San Fernando Cathedral,
Plaza de Islas, Military
Plaza, Governor's Palace

Mission Valero
(The Alamo)

Upper
Presido
Road

Salado
Creek

Leon
Creek

San
Pedro
Creek

Mission
Concepcion

Lower
Presidio
Road

Mission
San
Jose

Medina
River

Rosillo
Creek

Point known
as San Simon

Mission
San
Juan

To
Larado

To La
Bahia

Camino
Real

Mission
Espada

Garza's
Crossing

Cassin Crossing

Additional
Perez Grant
1808

Perez
Rancho

La
Barranca

San Antonio
River

To
Presidio de San
Juan Bautista

Perez
Crossing

Scale in miles
0 1 2 3

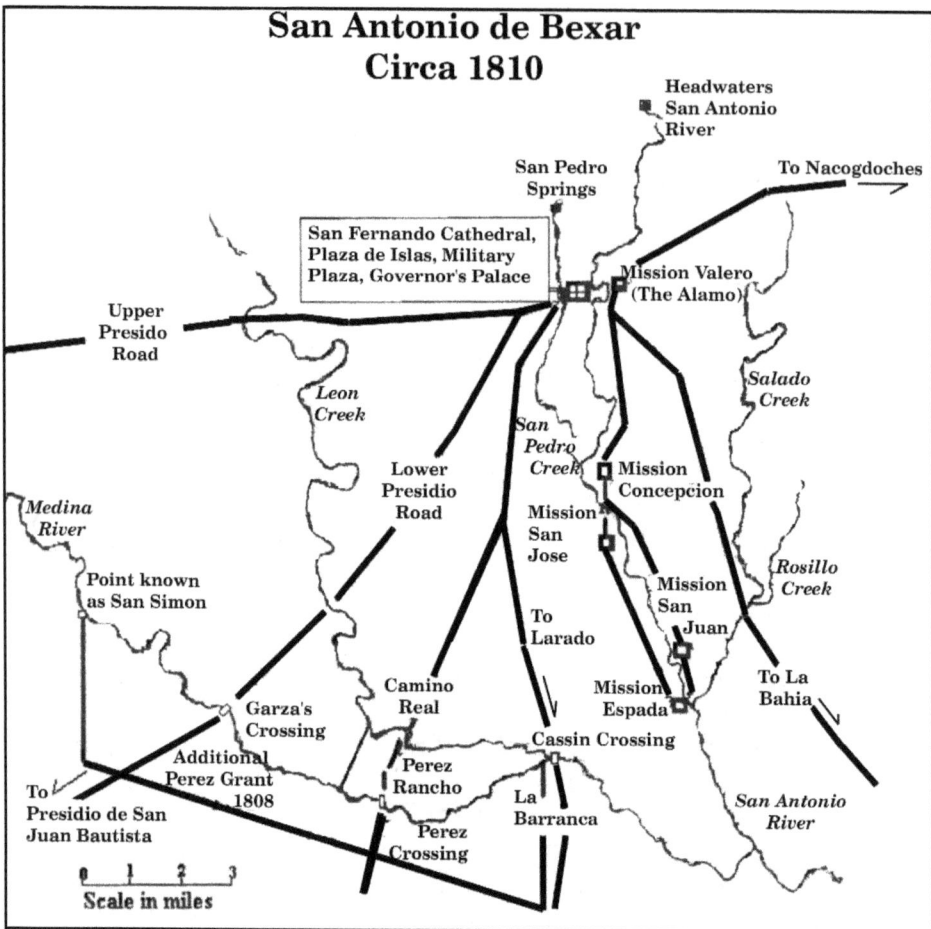

*Map of San Antonio de Bexar circa 1810
showing Pérez grants.*

Pérez was not only prospering, his popularity among the citizens and soldiers was growing. Some might say his popularity was due to the governor being his house guest. However, when Cordero was replaced as governor by Manuel Maria de Salcedo in September 1808, and allowed to return to his residence in Montelovez, Pérez still commanded respect. He was elected *sindico de ranchos* along the Medina River in 1809, a job made easier by the kinsmen who had acquired *ranchos* on the Medina and Leon. To help his son with ranching chores he purchased a slave, Jose de la Santa, from subdeacon Juan Manuel Zambrano, a flamboyant character who was soon to play a part in the political turbulence of San Antonio de Bexar. Pérez was still called to lead scouting expeditions, and his meticulous diaries of these expeditions can be found in the Bexar Archives.

Casas Revolt

The call for a revolution against the royalist government in Mexico City began in 1810, when a fifty-seven-year-old priest named Miguel Hidalgo y Costilla, from the village of Dolores in Guanajuato, sounded his call for independence. *"El Grito de Dolores,"* was the cry. "Long live independence and death to bad government." It was September 16.

By December the rebellion had reached the Rio Grande border of Texas. Salcedo was preparing to send Captain Pérez and the militia to the border in January. Pérez had already informed his men to prepare for the journey. Many of the soldiers were irritated by the prospect of leaving their families in midwinter. Furthermore, community leaders would be faced with mounting a civilian guard if the militia left town. *Alcalde* Francisco Travieso, representing the other *alcaldes* from villages surrounding San Antonio, called upon Juan Bautista de las Casas to lead a revolt against Governor Salcedo. Casas was a retired militia captain from Nuevo Santander and was living in San Antonio.

Casas willingly accepted the call and with help from disgruntled members of the militia arrested a surprised Salcedo and Herrera, the garrison commandant, January 22, 1811. Casas and his cohorts, espousing home rule and following the *"grito"* of Hidalgo, said European-born Spaniards, called *gachupines,* were not acceptable as leaders. Of some importance in assessing the passive role of

Captain Pérez in the revolt are actions of two militia lieutenants, Francisco Ignacio Escamilla and Antonio Saenz.
Both had been jailed by Salcedo before the revolt as revolutionary agents and perhaps had undermined Pérez'
authority within the militia. After the revolt, Casas had
the lieutenants released. He then sent Lieutenant Saenz
and *alcalde* Gavino Delgado to lead a body of militia to
Nacogdoches and establish a revolutionary government.

Casas' ruling junta wisely kept Captain Pérez at
home, asking him to prepare a report on supplies needed
for the four militia companies in Texas. Pérez was too well
liked to arrest and known to be staunchly Royalist. When
Saenz and Delgado returned, Casas had Saenz arrested
for alleged theft of monies confiscated from *gachupines* in
Nacogdoches. Once the Nacogdoches expedition returned, Pérez, his brother-in-law Francisco Ruiz (the
teacher), and the colorful archdeacon Juan Manuel Zambrano were convinced Casas did not have support of the
people and plotted a counter-coup. Zambrano was chosen
to lead the counter-coup, with support from *alcalde*
Delgado. Casas was ousted March 2, 1811. Pérez easily
convinced the wayward militia to join the counter coup
and was named a member of the new junta, having nim-
bly walked the tightrope of loyalty to ad interim governor
Casas, and his allegiance to the crown. In the meantime,
Hidalgo had been captured and was executed in the city
of Chihuahua, July 30, 1811.

In June 1811, Captain Pérez traveled to Nacogdoches
with reinforcements and money for the outpost, courtesy
of the new junta. When Governor Salcedo and Command-
ante Herrera returned to San Antonio, Pérez was not punished for his service to Casas after the revolt, but reward-
ed for leadership in the counter-coup. For loyalty to the
crown, Villa San Antonio de Bejar became Ciudad San
Antonio de Bejar.

The ranch on the Medina still drew his attention, but
more and more Pérez was occupied with official business,
meeting with Indian groups, and chasing renegades and
outlaws. He met with Comanche leader Cordero (not to be
confused with Antonio Cordero) during February 1812.

If 1812 seemed to be a year of military action, one family event restored a balance. Pérez' son, Jose Ignacio, married Maria Josefa Cortinas on May 30. The Pérez home on Military Plaza was a festive place as the wedding celebration moved from the church to the bridegroom's town home. A dance on the promenade continued far into the night.

Trouble was brewing in the east. A band of Hidalgo followers, led by Bernardo Gutierrez de Lara, and some American adventurers, led by Augustus Magee, united to march on Spanish forces in Texas. The initial success of the Gutierrez-Magee expedition, and inability of the central government to spare Veteran Royalist forces, spurred Governor Salcedo to engage the rebels at the Presidio La Bahia. After keeping the rebels (Republicans) penned up in the old fortress for several months, Salcedo decided to return to San Antonio, more because of desertions than combat losses. The Republican Army was hot on the heels of Salcedo's forces. Gen. Simon de Herrera, Salcedo's military commandant, decided to ambush the Republicans at Rosillo Creek.[17] Herrera's forces were out-gunned and fled toward San Antonio.

Governor Salcedo, who had been treated reasonably well when exiled by Casas, expected the best of his adversaries and surrendered to the Gutierrez-Magee forces in San Antonio. They held him prisoner for a short time. Then, under the guise of taking him to a neutral area, Salcedo was murdered along with Herrera and other loyalist officers by Gutierrez and a cohort, Captain Delgado.

Captain Pérez escaped the roundup that followed Salcedo's surrender in San Antonio. He managed to join Lt. Col. Ignacio Elizondo's Spanish Royalist unit and fought at the battle of Alazan, June 20, 1813. The early morning attack at Alazan by a smaller Republican force sent Elizondo's troops scattering and brought considerable embarrassment to Royalists. Pérez continued riding with Elizondo to join forces with a larger division moving northward from Laredo, this one led by one-eyed Gen. Joaquin de Arredondo.

Battle of Medina

The Battle of Medina was fought in August 1813. It took place just south and east of the Pérez ranch. Fifty-two-year-old Juan Ignacio Pérez, by then a very senior captain, served under General Arredondo in the decisive battle against the Americans and rebel Mexicans. One of several officers acquainted with the area, Pérez and others presumably counseled General Arredondo to cross the Medina below its confluence with Leon Creek. The Camino Real route crossing his ranch was being watched, and would require the army to ford both the Medina and Leon Creek, then negotiate the steep north banks which would become muddy and slippery as the army crossed. Of lesser consequence, Juan Ignacio's stone house was on a high point just west of the route the Camino Real took across his ranch. A fight at Pérez Crossing might have endangered his house, Jose Ignacio's family, and what little remained of his sun-scorched crops.

From the story as told by Ted Schwarz and Robert Thonhoff (see *Battle of Medina, Forgotten Battlefield of the First Texas Revolution*), it appears the crossing at the Garza ranch, or Laredo road crossing, was Arredondo's destination prior to the engagement. Both crossings were below the Pérez ranch.

Juan Ignacio was one of eighty-one cited for bravery during the battle and given a gold medal by Arredondo. He wore the medal proudly pinned on the band of his broad-brimmed *sombrero,* to the chagrin of rebel Bexar residents. Quashing the "Republican Army" did not quash the spirit of independence among some of the Mexican populace who remained. The medal is round with a multi-pointed star on one side. It has a Lion of Castile centered inside the star with the inscription, *"Vencio en Tejas el 18 de Agosto de 1813,"* translated: "He conquered in Texas on August 18, 1813." The medal is still in the possession of the family and was worn by Ed Walsh on several public occasions. A little known cadet (third) lieutenant, Antonio Lopez de Santa Anna, also fought at Me-

Battle of Medina medal is shown here worn by Ed Walsh, a fifth-generation descendant of Colonel Pérez.

dina under the flag of Spain and received an identical medal. Santa Anna, as most know, returned to San Antonio twenty-three years later as commander of the Mexican Army and laid siege to the Alamo.

Following the rout at Medina River, Pérez led patrols pursuing Indians who had fought with the rebels, riding with Colonel Elizondo as far as the Trinity River. Elizondo continued to Nacogdoches and Pérez returned to a devastated San Antonio. Arredondo assigned him the task of looking after properties of the fleeing rebels and to file reports on those who surrendered. The toll on San Antonio in the aftermath of the battle was far reaching. The Spanish army extracted revenge for the deaths of Salcedo and Herrera. Shortages of food, missing family members, a breakdown in municipal services, and pesky Indians, all contributed to a disheartened population.

The competence of Pérez in restoring a semblance of peace and order, and the shortage of other qualified candidates, resulted in requests he again serve as *alcalde*. Formally requesting exemption from serving in that capacity, he dodged an onerous task at this point in the history of San Antonio. The purge of community leadership that followed the Battle of Medina was the severest hindrance to recovery.

Don Juan Ignacio Pérez was mentioned in General Arredondo's report of the battle[18] and later was promoted to lieutenant colonel for his "role in the restoration of Royalist authority in Texas."[19] He continued to divide his time between the Governor's Palace and Rancho de la Purisima Concepción. It was a bittersweet promotion for Juan Ignacio. His neighbor and brother-in-law, Francisco Ruiz, had been a colonel in the Guiterrez-Magee Republican army and was not given amnesty by General Arredondo. Ruiz owned the land west of the Pérez ranch on the Medina and was an uncle of Jose Angel Navarro, who owned the ranch north of him. Because of the stature of Ruiz in the community and in the rebel force, his land was confiscated. Despite the pitiful condition of ranches in the area, the Pérez ranch continued to survive favored as it was by both Leon Creek and the Medina River.

In 1814, Juan and Clemencia's eldest daughter, twenty-three-year-old *doña* Maria Gertrudis Pérez, became the bride of Brig. Gen. *don* Antonio Cordero, then sixty-two years old and residing in Coahuila as commandant of military forces.[20] *Doña* Maria was a bright and energetic young woman, shrewd in business dealings, and a striking beauty. Her interest in the ranch was minimal and before her marriage she took care of family business interests in town. As the wife of the brigadier, she wore his title well and often reviewed the Coahuilan troops in his absence.

When Mariano Varela was replaced as temporary governor of Texas in 1816, Pérez served as interim governor of Texas until Manuel Pardo arrived to fill that position. He was perhaps the first native Texan to serve as governor. Indians continued to be a problem for the residents of Texas, and Pérez was frequently called upon to negotiate with headmen and chiefs to prevent conflict. His reports of Indian attacks, and munitions used by the militia, are filed in the Bexar Archives along with other official documents of his tenure as temporary governor.

The year 1817 was a busy one for the governor of Spanish Texas and commander of the militias. After transferring the office of governor to Pardo in March, he plunged into the pursuit of renegades, making several successful expeditions to recover stock stolen from local ranches. While on an expedition in April, Pérez was ordered to return to Bexar because of an imminent attack by Indians. There was no attack, perhaps because Pérez had returned, and in May he led an expedition to the frontier (most likely the Rio Grande area). He was given the title of "commandant of the cavalry" upon his return. A meeting with the Vidais Indians took place west of San Antonio in August. Pérez and his troops returned from that parley with a supply of ammunition he received from Presidio San Juan Bautista on the Rio Grande.

Meanwhile, Col. Henry Perry of the ill-fated Gutierrez-Magee expedition had gathered a small force and tried to assault the Presidio La Bahia in June 1817.

Though Perry was defeated, the governor concluded a stronger force was needed to deter other rebels. Perhaps the colonel's popularity influenced Pardo to get Pérez out of town. Ever the loyal officer and trouble shooter, Pérez was sent to La Bahia in September 1817. In October he was given command of Presidio La Bahia. One of the first things Pérez did was lead an expedition to the Matagorda port, reasserting Spanish influence along the coast. His willingness to serve was tested in this assignment, and in April 1818 he sent a formal request for his family to be allowed to join him. He seemed impressed by the prospects of having a ranch in the lush coastal pastures surrounding La Bahia, and wanted to distance himself from the pressures and politics of San Antonio de Bexar.

Whatever his reasoning, the resulting order from the new governor, Antonio Maria Martinez, was to return to Bexar and transfer command of La Bahia to Capt. Jose de Jesus Aldrete. Pérez was too influential in Bexar to exile him at the La Bahia outpost.

Returning to Bexar, charges were brought against him for insulting a citizen named Ignacio Chavez. For this Pérez was jailed. What a disgraceful end this would have been to his career in today's military. But the early *Bexarenos* were a litigious society and filed charges for most anything that displeased them. Many of the Canary Islanders and their descendants spent time in the Bexar jail for seemingly petty offenses. Released three days later and restored to command of the militia, Pérez resumed his efforts to defend the outlying areas. For his service to the Crown, he received several letters from General Arredondo expressing gratitude.

Life on Rancho de la Purísima Concepción was testing the mettle of thirty-two-year-old Jose Ignacio. Maria Josefa had given him three sons and three daughters to help on the ranch. The extended absence of his father, more than 20,000 acres of grazing land to protect from cattle thieves and Indians, and community responsibilities kept him busy. He had only a few hired hands, one slave, and his sons, who were too young to be of much help.

The James Long Invasion

Several years after the battle of Medina, while Pérez still commanded the Spanish militia garrison in San Antonio, Governor Antonio Maria Martinez sent him to drive Dr. James Long and his expeditionary force out of Texas.[21] A medical doctor from Natchez, Mississippi, Long was convinced by the ousted rebel leader Bernardo Gutierrez that Texas was his for the taking. Born in Virginia and raised in Tennessee, Long gathered up a group of adventurers and moved into Spanish territory establishing his capital at Nacogdoches June 23, 1819. The self-proclaimed general had heard of the weakness of the Spanish Army and decided to exploit that weakness.

Normally the San Antonio garrison only defended settlements within a 200-mile radius, such as La Bahia. But, the Spanish Army was straining to contain unrest in Mexico. It could little afford to launch the army on an expedition to the frontier of New Spain and risk loss of the interior. General Arredondo knew there was a man in Bexar he could call upon. Colonel Pérez was spending more time as a rancher than soldier after hearing his son's plea for help. He could lead the march against Long.

With more than 500 men under his command, Colonel Pérez (called General Pérez by T. R. Fehrenbach in *Lone Star*) left San Antonio in September 1819, and made a physically punishing ride up El Camino Real to Nacogdoches. They fought grass fires started by Indians loyal to Long, and took prisoners along the way. Pérez fought small detachments of Long's men on October 11 and October 15, arriving in the pine forests of Nacogdoches October 28. From there he moved further to the Sabine in the "neutral" ground between Texas and Louisiana. Pérez' troops scattered Long's 600-man army and returned to San Antonio with some captives along a now muddy El Camino Real, reaching San Antonio February 2, 1820.

The cold, damp weather put Juan Ignacio in bed, ill enough to have a last will and testament prepared later that year. (See Appendix B.) Such was the concern over the little colonel's illness that General Arredondo, his military patron, sent him a letter with instructions on how to combat his illness. Making his recovery more difficult were the reports he had to file on prisoners taken, confiscated property, captured horses, and detailed expense accounts. More than thirty entries are filed in the Bexar Archives concerning that expedition.

When Mexico achieved independence from Spanish rule June 30, 1821, Pérez and other civil and military leaders throughout the province of Texas gathered in San Antonio to swear allegiance to the new government headed by Augustin de Iturbide. Jose Angel Navarro, son of Corsican merchant Angel Navarro and older brother of Jose Antonio Navarro (Texas patriot), was designated by the Iturbide government to accept the transfer of power from Governor Martinez. Navarro most likely performed the swearing in ceremony. Pérez retained his commission as a lieutenant colonel in the Mexican militia and little else changed in the province. Indians continued to harass the outlying settlements and Anglo squatters continued to enter the Mexican state via Louisiana.

Meanwhile, Long was plotting a reentry into Texas. Gathering another army, he established camp at Point Bolivar across from Galveston Island and not far from the pirate Lafitte's headquarters. On September 19, 1821, he sailed down the Gulf Coast from Galveston and marched unopposed to Goliad. Long quickly captured the fortress of La Bahia. When the newly appointed Mexican governor heard of Long's coup, he called on the "old colonel," a title often used by Juan Ignacio's descendants, to again rid the territory of Long.

Under the flag of Mexico this time, and with only a few hundred men, Pérez left his home on the Military Plaza carrying the statue of the Blessed Virgin. He met Long at Presidio La Bahia and laid siege. After a smattering of shots hit the fort, Pérez, now faithfully representing the new Mexican government, arranged Long's surrender. Family tradition says Juan Ignacio talked Long into surrendering. Other accounts accuse Pérez of trickery in getting Long to surrender. (See *Presidio La Bahia,* by Kathryn Stoner O'Connor.) Perhaps both accounts have elements of truth. The "old colonel" had laid siege to La Bahia before with Herrera in charge. Now that he was in command, he ended the confrontation quickly and without loss of life.

Juan Ignacio returned to his San Antonio home perhaps realizing this was his last expedition. Though in poor health he made several trips to the ranch in 1822. He was still recognized as the leading cattleman in the area, although Jose was doing most of the work. The outings were therapeutic, but the many campaigns, forced marches, and hours on horseback took their toll. He made one last extended trip of a personal nature. His son-in-law, Antonio Cordero, died in the spring of 1823. Pérez made the trip to Durango and escorted his daughter back to San Antonio.

Juan Ignacio died in October 1823, at the age of sixty-two and was buried in the Purisima Concepción Chapel of San Fernando Cathedral. So ended the life of the founder of Rancho de la Purísima Concepción, surrounded by his family which included a boy rescued from the Comanches and other adopted children. An honor guard of his militia stood by. It could be said of him, he combined a good name with much wealth, a fulfillment of the benediction Maria Pérez de Casanova had placed on her sons' heads 100 years earlier.

Chapter Four

Jose Ignacio Pérez, The Next Generation

At the time Juan Ignacio Pérez died, he was the wealthiest man in the province. Among the significant items were his ranch properties, houses of wood and stone construction throughout the town, numerous land and water rights in the upper and lower *labors* (fields), thirty-eight mules and numerous horses, and nearly 10,000 pesos in cash. A thorough reading of Don Juan Ignacio Pérez de Casanova's will impresses one with his generosity and thoughtfulness. The provision and care of his adoptive children, acknowledging his wife's contribution to the accumulation of their joint wealth, his charity toward the church, and kindness toward his slave, mark him as a most unusual man.

Jose Ignacio Pérez inherited the bulk of his father's estate. Though he had spent most his life farming and running cattle on Rancho de la Purísima Concepción, Jose was an educated man, capable of handling the family business interests. Their substantial holdings needed frequent attention. Like his father, he was not an idle man and tended to matters on the ranch as well as looking after properties the family owned in town. Unlike his father, Jose had little interest in the militia or fighting. His passive stance in the politics of the day appeared to keep him out of trouble and during the turbulent years of Mexican rule Jose managed to increase his holdings.

Doña Maria Gertrudis and her husband, Antonio

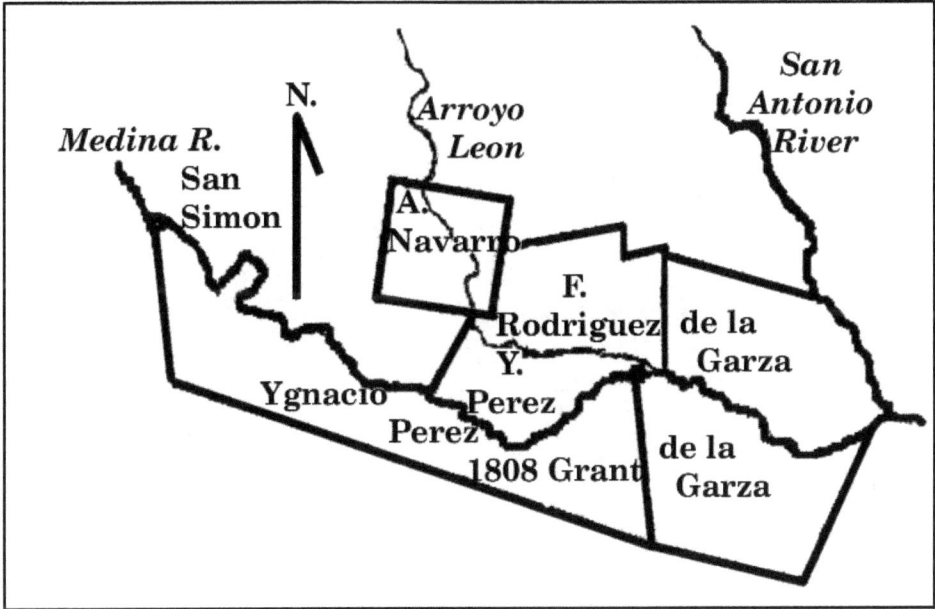

Ranches on the Medina.

Cordero, had previously received a 2,000-peso loan from the Colonel Pérez "old colonel." Gertrudis received the balance due on the loan as part of her settlement, along with other properties in town. *Doña* Concepción and her husband, Fernando Rodriquez, used 1,680 pesos from her inheritance to buy a large tract of land north of Leon Creek, adjacent to Juan Ignacio's grant.

Although Juan Ignacio left the house on Military Plaza to his son, Jose preferred living on the ranch and allowed Gertrudis to stay in the house on Military Plaza with their mother. Gertrudis lived there until after her mother's death then married Italian businessman Jose Cassiano. The Cassianos moved to the old Jose Pérez homestead on Dolorosa Street, a prominent location near the cathedral and part of Gertrudis' inheritance.[22] Gertrudis died of an illness in 1832. Her inheritance from her father became part of the Cassiano estate. However, a medallion she wore on ceremonial occasions while mar-

Photo of Concepción Linn Walsh wearing a medallion
originally belonging to Gertrudis. A flaming sword of inlaid
gold is the center of the medallion.

ried to Brigadier General Cordero has been passed down through the Walsh family. A royalist to the end, she had her will be constructed to preclude the Mexican government from " . . . getting their hands on any of her assets," according to family members. She is entombed in the San Fernando Cathedral and is the only Peres (Pérez) with a stone marker in the present-day cathedral.[23]

American settlers had begun to arrive in 1825 and were allowed to possess property by taking Mexican citizenship and professing to be Catholic. One of the desired effects of this new policy was to establish a protective barrier between Bexar and the marauding plains Indians. Despite the new settlers, raids on San Antonio and nearby ranches continued unabated. A servant of Jose Ignacio was murdered by Indians in 1827.

Jose Ignacio became more isolated because of his loyalty to the central government. Among his neighbors and the new settlers arriving, a ground swell of independence was growing. There was nothing rebellious about Jose. He tended to business and was granted a license to provide Bexar with meat in 1833. When Ben Milam and his followers entered San Antonio in 1835, battling the Mexican army led by Santa Anna's brother-in-law, General Cos, Jose Ignacio began making arrangements to leave the area. An acceptable practice in that time for people leaving their properties unattended was the use of an agent, or property manager. Jose Ignacio appointed several persons to look after his properties, inform him if taxes were due and the amount, and collect rents. As was the Spanish custom he notified municipal authorities of his pending departure, including the new *alcalde* and relative, Francisco Antonio Ruiz, the son of Jose Francisco.

Animosities had grown between the new settlers and the Spanish/Mexican majority. Peace-loving Jose Ignacio was threatened by none other than Erastus "Deaf" Smith, called "el Sordo" by his Spanish-speaking acquaintances, in late 1835 or early 1836. Smith had a cattle ranch south of Mission San Jose on the San Antonio River and perhaps resented the size and success of Jose Ignacio's land

Tax receipt given to "Ygnacio Perez" January 8, 1831. His state and county tax for 1830 amounted to $29.05, for: 4,428 acres of land; 15,284 acres of land; 10 lots in San Antonio; 5 horses, 542 cattle, and 250 sheep. Note it was written in English and dollars were the currency.

holdings on the Medina. After the rebel's defeat of General Cos in 1835, Smith was given an official role in the government and used his authority to oust Jose Ignacio. He told residents of San Antonio he had "chased Pérez and some other Mexicans" out of Bexar County. A bounty had allegedly been placed on their heads for being "centralists."

Whether from Deaf Smith's wild threats, or his sense of impending disaster, Jose Ignacio wisely took his family to Mexico and lived on the Rio Grande during the revolution and turbulent aftermath. He was in touch with family members, Concepción Pérez Rodriguez and his former brother-in-law Jose Cassiano. Friends were supposedly looking out for the ranch, but the distance and size of the ranch kept them from thorough inspection. Little did they suspect that squatters had settled on the south bank of the Medina and laid claim to that 16,000 acres. It was still a wild and mostly unpopulated area. Jose Ignacio continued paying taxes on his properties and his registered "agents" looked after his interests.[24] In 1838 the Samuel Mavericks were guests in the Cassianos' home, and visited the Pérez ranch "on the Camino Real," according to Maverick.

When Jose Ignacio first returned in 1846, he found the ranch being claimed by a new breed of Texans hoping to gain from the Republic's freewheeling land dealings. The open range laws were very profitable for procuring new, unbranded livestock and the lack of a good ranch manager, while the Pérez family was away, made them very susceptible to cattle rustlers. He waited until the conclusion of the war between Mexico and the United States before bringing his family back to San Antonio.

Settling themselves in the "Governor's Palace" on Military Plaza, Pérez and his family began putting their lives back in order. Undaunted by the legal windmill he was preparing to joust, Jose Ignacio began a protracted fight that eventually resulted in a ruling by the Texas Supreme Court in 1851. In the case of "Paschal and others V. Pérez and others" the court upheld Jose's title to the

New landowners south of the Medina.

original league of land but stripped him forever of the four leagues west of the Medina River.

Challenges to Spanish/Mexican land grants were a boon for lawyers. In the disputed area between the Nueces River and Rio Grande, the Bourland-Miller Commission was established to adjudicate claims. While many of the Spanish/Mexican grantees and their descendants were confirmed as the rightful owners, new Texans bought up the ranches as in the case of Llano Grande and Los Mesteños in the lower valley. The Antonio Rivas grant near Eagle Pass, dating to 1765, was refiled by heirs and was sold piece by piece to new Texans. William L. Cazneau, an officer in the Republic of Texas army, purchased the upper part of the Rivas grant in 1850. William Stone, the first judge of Maverick County, once owned part of the Rivas grant.[25]

The 16,000 acres of land south of the Medina that once belonged to the Pérez family straddled the key routes to Laredo and the Rio Grande Valley. In later years oil would be discovered on much of the land, and a catfish farmer would ignite another battle for the courts to settle. The new settlers were Alexas Bustillos, J. M. Daes, N. M. Dawson, Stephen Jett, Bruno Martinez, Sam McCulloch, Jr., F. E. Paschal, Henry Peace, Rufeno Rodriguez, Francisco Roten, Charles Yoacum, and others.[26]

Church services were still held in the small chapel begun by Jose's father, constructed northeast of the stone ranch house. The grounds around the chapel became a final resting place for many of the family and ranch hands. When Jose Ignacio died in 1852, he was buried inside the chapel on Rancho de la Purísima Concepción.[27] No doubt he still dreamed of his empire on the right bank of the Medina being restored. His will includes those properties as contested.

Chapter Five

Pérez y Linn Ranch

The will of Jose Ignacio was not settled until October of 1855, when Maria Josefa and her new husband asked the court to partition the property. Raven-haired Maria Josefa, beautiful and soon-to-be-wealthy in her own right, married a former school mate and businessman, Jacob Linn, in 1855. Her sisters, Trinidad and Concepción, remained spinsters and were actively involved with the ranch.

As the result of her marriage, the joint holdings of the daughters, including the ranch and the house on Military Plaza, were potential problems for the new couple. The request for partition resulted in a division of the property. To his daughters, Trinidad, Maria Josefa, and Concepción, Jose Ignacio gave each one-third of the ranch, or 1,390.5 acres each, to be precise. Each also received amounts of property in San Antonio and all shared in the "Governor's Palace."[28] His sons, Ignacio Sr. and Ignacio Jr., received small inheritances. Ignacio Sr. received 234.5 acres of the ranch on the Medina. His acreage was at the western end of the ranch as depicted earlier. He also received some land in the *labors,* part of the house on Military Plaza, a lot in San Antonio, and ten cows with calves. Ignacio Jr. (Ignacio the younger) received land in the *labors,* and a lot in the city. There was no mention of Jesus, the second born, in the will and perhaps he preceded his father in death.

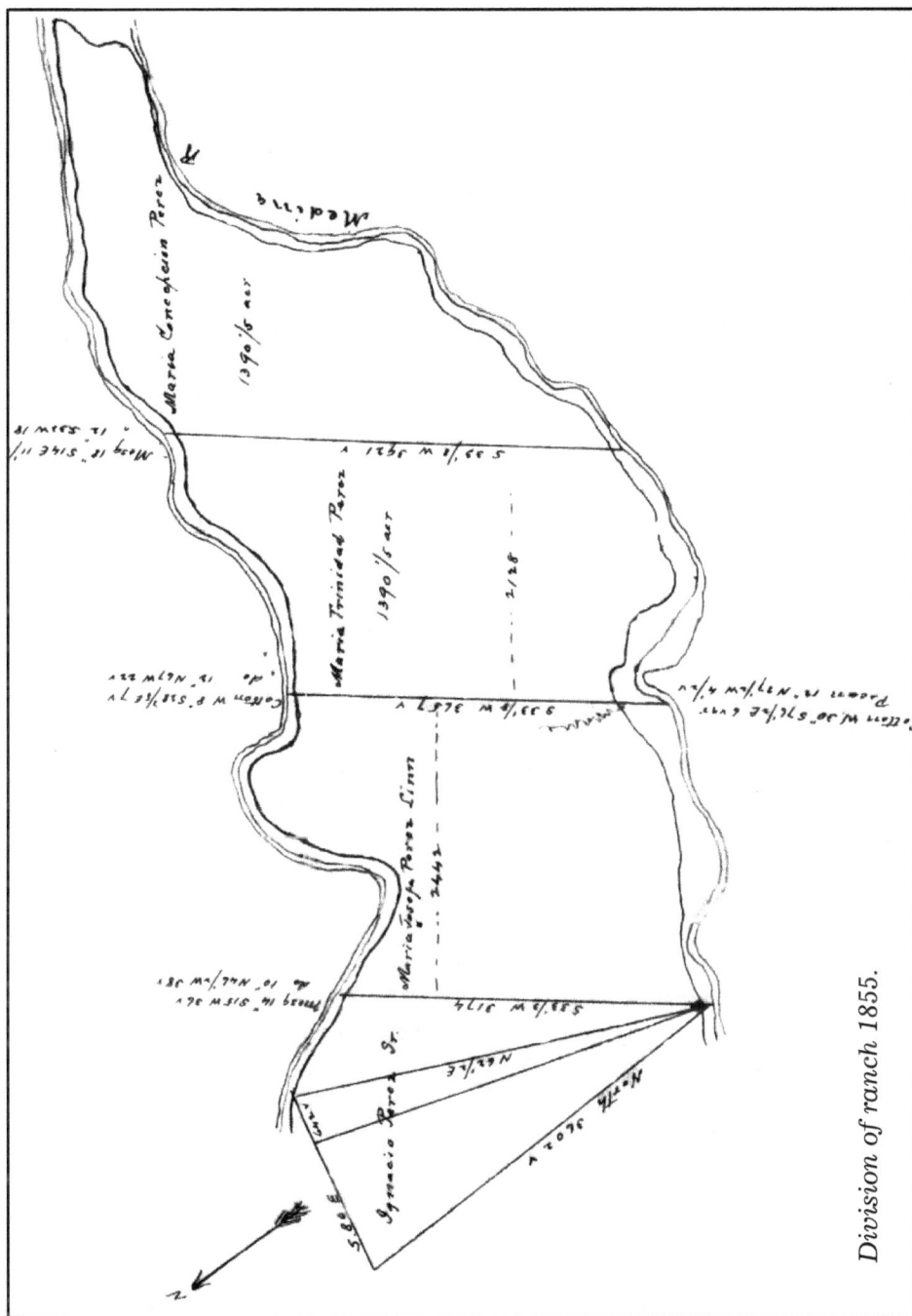

Division of ranch 1855.

N

Presidio Road - Commerce Street

Well

Josefa Cortinas

Ignacio Sr.

Trinidad Perez

Maria Josefa Perez Linn

Concepcion Perez

The property extended east to San Pedro Creek. Only the house was partitioned. The well and garden were maintained in common ownership.

Site of 1860 Court House

Plaza de Armas

Plaza de Armas (Military Plaza) was used as a market area during this period. The promenade in front of the Govenor's Palace was paved with stone and was shaded by live oaks. It was a popular meeting place.

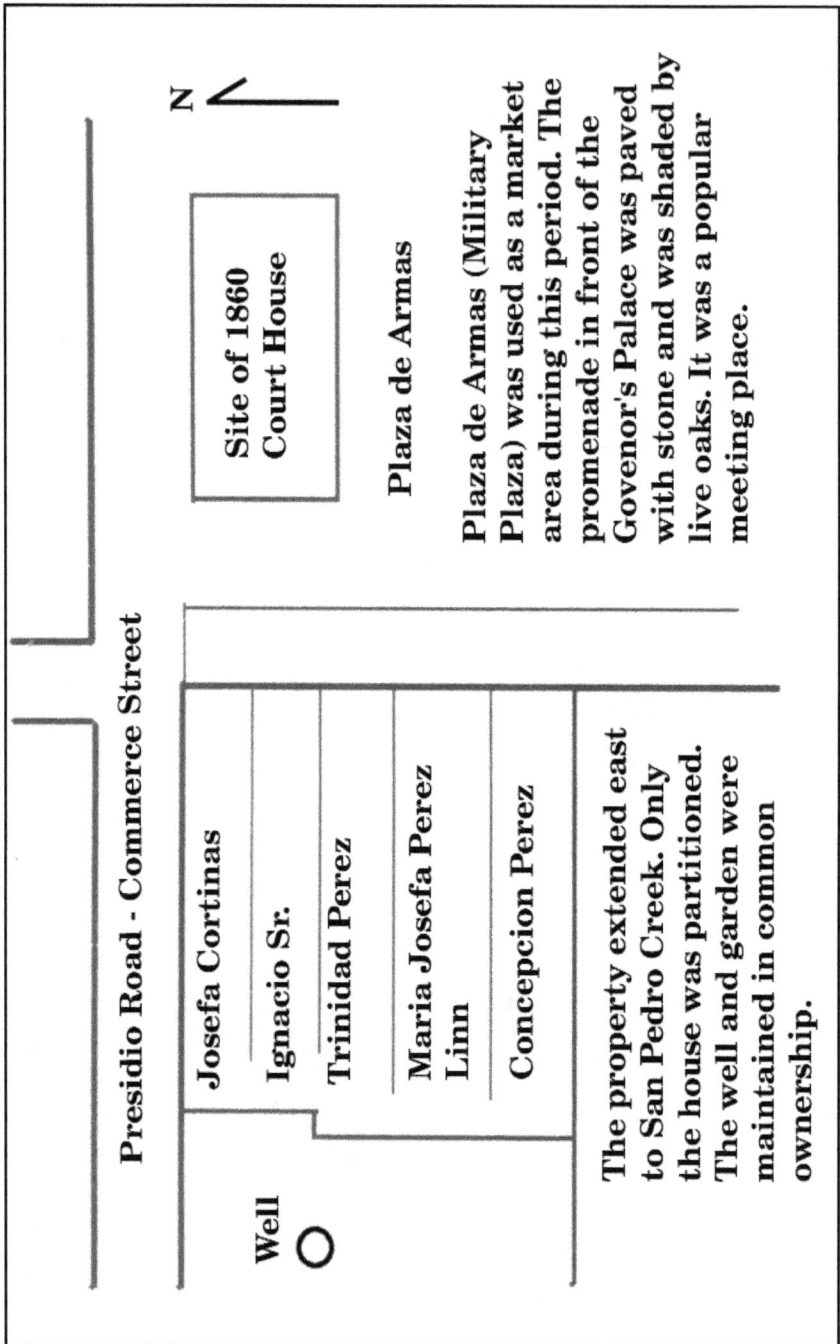

Division of Governor's Palace in 1855. Jose Ignacio wanted everyone to have part of the house and stipulated such in his will. The division took place in probate court at the Linns' insistence.

To his wife, Josefa Cortinas, he bequeathed a room in the house fronting Military Plaza, a portion of his land in the lower *labors*, a portion of land called *"Tabla de los Leales,"* and eight head of cattle and oxen.

This division of property was considered unique in that it gave each family member a suite of rooms in the house on Military Plaza. (See diagram opposite.) So unique was the division that Ripley's "Believe It or Not!" included a comment about the arrangement. It appeared in the April 7, 1958, issue of the *San Antonio Light:* "The Governor's Palace in San Antonio, Texas, Originally was the home of Ygnacio Perez—who bequeathed each of its rooms to a different member of the family." The division of the estate satisfied the Linns.

Jacob Linn was born in Egsweiler, Bavaria, November 30, 1825, to Daniel and Elizabeth Linn. In 1831, he accompanied his parents and sister on a voyage to Texas. His mother became ill and died during the voyage and was buried at sea. Linn's father died when they reached Port Lavaca. Orphaned and without relatives in Texas, Jacob and his sister were brought to San Antonio by some good-hearted fellow passengers.[29] The German Linns were apparently not related to the Irish Linns living in Victoria. A short time after arriving in San Antonio, Jacob's sister died and he was adopted in 1833 by Father Francisco Maynes. Maynes was a supernumerary (extra) chaplain in San Fernando Cathedral and insured Jacob had the finest education available in the province.

Educated in Spanish and English, Linn was considered brilliant by his teachers, and unusually talented with his hands. He learned the gunsmith trade working as an apprentice. Perhaps the most skilled gunsmith in San Antonio, Linn maintained a well-supplied shop on the Military Plaza across from the Governor's Palace. Upon Father Maynes' death, Jacob inherited a sizeable estate. His newfound wealth allowed him to devote more time and expense to the artistry of gun making, including silver and gold inlay. In his youth he attended school with the Pérez children before their flight to Mexico, and even visited in their home. He found the dark-haired Maria Josefa even more attractive upon her return from Mexico. It is said he never knew when he began loving Maria, perhaps from their first meeting.

After their wedding in 1855, Jacob and Josefa moved into their portion of the Governor's Palace, where their children were born. Maria Josefa had two daughters, Maria Isabel de la Trinidad (born December 14, 1855) and Casamira de la Concepción Linn y Pérez (born March 4, 1868). A son, Jacob, died as an infant. The daughters were named, in part, to honor Josefa's sisters. Torn between town and ranching interests since the early 1860s, and spurred by the 1867 outbreak of cholera in San Antonio, Jacob built a thirteen-room, wooden house on his wife's portion of the ranch. It was more modern and comfortable than the stone house built by Colonel Pérez, which by this time was no longer usable as a residence. (A photograph of the house taken in the early 1900s shows it had a "Texas" porch circling the house. The Linn chapel could be seen in the background.)

Their home was completed in 1868, shortly after the birth of Concepción. It was located west of present-day Applewhite Road and north of Watson Road, near Leon Creek. In one room stood an altar, and along one wall, in a niche, was the statue Colonel Pérez had rescued from Las Cabras. Initially they used this room for their church services since they were four or five miles from Espada Mission, the nearest church. A priest would come and spend the night with them once a month. The next day he would say mass for the family and workers, then return to the mission. Eventually Jacob built a chapel near their ranch house, on land owned by Josefa. The stone and stucco chapel had wood encased gothic windows, quite rare and artistic for a ranch chapel.

The Linn daughters were taught on the ranch by a private teacher. Eventually they were each taken into San Antonio for school. Concepción, a slender and striking young lady, later took art training at a convent in Victoria.

Jacob applied himself to learning the cattle business.

Photo of Ed Walsh at the Texas A&M branding wall with his wife and daughter.

He raised cotton, corn, and cane; and, though fences were nonexistent, ran large herds of cattle and horses on the spread owned by his wife and her two sisters. During branding time, a well-equipped chuck wagon accompanied Jacob and his cowhands as they scoured surrounding counties for the branded stallions and their *"manadas."* It was still the era of open range and the JLC brand, shared by Jacob and his sister-in-law, Concepción, had to be burned on the cheek, or flank, of each colt as early as possible. They used a small version of the brand for their horses and the large brand (see photo page 77) was used on cattle. When Concepción Pérez died, she willed her third of the ranch to her sister, Trinidad. The JLC brand is still used by the family and appears on cat-

Cattle at ranch.

tle in the accompanying photograph. It is the oldest brand still used in Bexar County. The Linn horses were in demand by circuses because of breeding practices that gave the Linns large numbers of matched horses.

Both Jacob and Josefa enjoyed horseback riding and hunting. Josefa's rifle was among the finest Jacob had produced in his shop. They hunted deer, turkey, and javelina, on horseback, with Josefa riding side-saddle. The ranch maintained a blacksmith shop, brick kiln, and commissary. With all the amenities the Linns brought to the ranch, it was like a small community. South of the Medina, the Applewhites were developing their ranch and farming enterprise. They had arrived in Texas about 1853 and brought slaves with them. After the Civil War, both the Linns and Applewhites began using sharecroppers. The Applewhites were the first in the area to use this form of labor on their large farm.

As Jacob grew older, he developed another hobby,

One of the fine horses still raised on the ranch.

still using the artistry of his hands. He turned to wood carving. Some family members recall seeing doll furniture in the Walsh home on Applewhite Road purported to be Jacob's work.

After only ten years on the ranch, fifty-three-year-old Jacob became ill and died, December 8, 1878. He was buried in the Pérez ranch chapel alongside his father-in-law. It remained for Josefa to decide who would inherit her third of the ranch. After twenty-eight-year-old Trinidad married Santiago Herrera in 1883, a male heir was born and named Jacob. Josefa adopted her grandson while he was still an infant and raised him as her own son until her death in 1889. Jacob (sometimes called Jacobo) was given the Linn name and inherited his maternal grandmother's third of the ranch. After Josefa's death, he was placed in the guardianship of his aunt, Concepción Linn. An undated document in the possession of the Walsh family has an extract of Josefa's will bequeathing to Hacobo (Jacobo) Linn, the son of Josefa's daughter Trinidad, her third of the ranch once he reached the age of twenty-one. In the meantime, that third of the ranch was to "belong to and be controlled by Concepción Linn."

Henry Burl Ross

Concepción later relied heavily on a former slave, who arrived on the ranch during the Civil War, to provide some continuity in ranch management. Henry Burl Ross (called Bur and Uncle Bur), an eighteen-year-old ex-slave, came to the Pérez-Linn Ranch in the early 1860s. One story of his arrival at the ranch was that his grandmother was leased by the Linns from Asa Mitchell. Accompanied by his grandmother and two brothers, he worked several years on the ranch to support his family. When the war ended, Bur got wanderlust and left to drive the big freight wagons going west. His brothers, Henry and Frank, stayed at the ranch and eventually became Linn's top cowhands.

When Bur returned to the ranch in the spring of 1868, he announced he was back to stay. And stay he did, for the next eighty-six years. First as houseboy and carriage driver for Josefa and the children, and later as cowhand and manager of the stock after Jacob's death.

Concepción Linn was only three weeks old when Bur returned to the ranch, and she later told many that she could not remember a day without "Uncle Bur" being in her home. He was an excellent cook and when Concepción married, Bur moved into her household and became part of her family. Bur lived on the ranch until his death September 21, 1953. He was buried in the family plot at San Fernando II Cemetery after a funeral service in the Walsh Ranch Chapel. The chapel at that time was in the Walsh home on Applewhite Road.

Picture of Burl Ross with Caroline and Patricia Walsh.

The abundance of cattle being driven to rail heads flooded the market with low-priced beef. But a new form of prosperity was just around the corner for Concepción.

*One of several tenant house structures still standing in 1990 on
Walsh ranch.*

In 1886, a rancher named Dullnig struck oil while drilling
for water in southeast Bexar County. The well is reputed
to be the first oil well in Texas. The same year oil was
found on the Linn-Pérez Ranch near the Applewhite Road
crossing of Leon Creek. C. A. Warner, in "Texas Oil and
Gas Since 1543," notes that production on the "F. T.
Walsh" ranch was reported in statistical tables in 1886.
Perhaps Frank Walsh owned a ranch in 1886, before marrying into the Linn family. If Warner was referring to the
well on the Linn-Pérez Ranch, Walsh did not enter the
picture until later, a minor technicality. However, wells
are still operating on ranch property, adjacent to, and on,
land condemned by the city for a reservoir.

Life on the ranch continued even without a male heir.
Bur and the other hands managed the cattle and horses,
and a blacksmith named Frank Hamer moved his young

family into one of the tenant (sharecropper) houses. Hamer was a former cavalry blacksmith who had married Lou Emma Francis and initially settled in the community of Fairview, near Floresville.[30] His son, Francis Augustus Hamer, became a captain in the Texas Rangers. As a ranger, Hamer was involved in many cases, including pursuit of the infamous Clyde Barrow and his girlfriend Bonnie. Hamer planned the ambush that ended the murderous careers of Bonnie and Clyde.

Chapter Six

Pérez, Linn y Walsh Ranch

In 1891, after the deaths of both her sister and mother, Concepción Linn and her ward, Jacob, were the sole heirs of the ranch. Concepción had been properly courted by Francis (Frank) Thomas Walsh, the son of an Irish-immigrant construction family. On November 5, 1891, Concepción and Frank were married. He was a rancher, perhaps owning a ranch with producing oil wells, and had experience in contracting and construction. Frank was a man of boundless energy, eager to bring this historic ranch into the twentieth century. Receiving two-thirds of the original ranch from her great-aunts, Trinidad and Concepción, for five dollars and love and consideration, Concepción and Frank ran the ranch as a family operation. The third of the ranch willed by Maria Josefa to her grandchild (and adopted son), Jacob Linn, was also managed by Frank and Concepción. They were the court appointed guardians of Jacob. As Jacob grew older, his distrust of his guardians also grew and soon he became estranged from the family.

Lawsuits followed concerning Jacob's share of the ranch and, once settled, 1,000 acres on the western portion of the ranch, reaching to State Highway 16, were no longer in the family. Jacob, according to family members, squandered his inheritance and died when he was only twenty-six years old. Ironically, Jacob's distrust had started over his share of the annual pecan crop gathered from the giant trees along the Medina River bank.

Concepción Linn about the time of her marriage in the 1890s.

Frank and Concepción had seven children. They were Mary, Anita, Lottie, Bessie, Francis T., Jr., Harry J., and Edward Patrick (Ed). For many years they lived in the Linn home and several of their children were born there. As the relationship with Jacob became intractable, Frank and Concepción built a home on the east side of Applewhite Road, including a chapel in their residence.

The Walsh Ranch Chapel was the site of a baptism March 3, 1978, and this is the last known group photograph of the Walsh siblings. Left to right: Lottie Walsh Mahla, Father Eustace Struckhoff, Mary Claude Walsh, Harry Walsh, Bessie Walsh, Frank Jr., Anita Walsh, and Edward Walsh.

Among the items Concepción had inherited was the family residence on Military Plaza, along with a number of other commercial and residential properties in San Antonio. She eventually sold the "Governor's Palace" to the City of San Antonio in 1929 for $55,000. Photos of the Walsh family at the transfer of ownership are in the May 3, 1932, issue of the *San Antonio Express*. The city restored the early nineteenth century home of the Pérez family and allowed visitors to wander through the furnished rooms of the "Governor's Palace" for a small fee. Social events sponsored by the mayor take place in the walled garden at the rear of the home.

Walsh Posse-Frank Walsh, Sr. is standing on the porch of their home on Applewhite Road. On horseback, (left to right) George W. Saunders on Zack; Edward Walsh on Amos; Frank Walsh, Jr. on an unnamed horse; Harry Walsh on Dun Mare; and Cecil Walsh on Blue. Saunders used this photograph on his Livestock Commission Company calendar in the 1920s. Cecil Walsh was a nephew Frank Sr. adopted.

One of their new neighbors on the Medina around the turn of the century was A. J. Swearingen, who owned a ranch on the south bank of the Medina near Oak Island. A. J. would fuss and fume that his son, Judson, was always tinkering and not working the farm or ranch like Walsh's sons. Judson attended school a few years at Oak Island, riding his horse to school, and taking his sister Nell over to the Walsh home on Applewhite Road for piano lessons. Anita Walsh was an accomplished pianist and gave lessons at the ranch house. Judson became good friends with the Walsh boys and spent many leisure hours riding horseback along the Medina River with Frank Jr. He even named his one-eyed mustang "Frank," after his friend.[31]

Judson Swearingen is part of this story because his roots were on the Medina. He was a brilliant young man, attending the University of Texas, earning a doctorate in chemical engineering, and teaching there while starting a business. He later worked as an inventor and, in the 1940s, was hired by the government to work on the "Manhattan Project." During one of his return visits to the Medina River in the early 1900s, Judson and the Walsh boys built themselves a two-way radio at the Walsh ranch house so Judson could keep in touch with his scientific world. At that time there was limited telephone service in the area. Later, he recalled, there was a "party" line and once it rang everyone listened in on the conversation.

From World War I until the start of World War II, the Walsh family provided a fine breed of matched horses for the U.S. Cavalry and the "tinkerer," Swearingen, helped develop the atomic bomb that ended World War II. Their contributions to the war effort were at both ends of the technology spectrum. Judson never forgot his ranching friends on the Medina, calling and visiting with his friend, Frank, into the 1970s. Swearingen is now incapacitated and resides in a San Antonio health care facility.

Edward and his brothers shared responsibilities on the ranch in the early years. Frank Jr. was overseer of the farming operation while Harry and Edward ran the cattle business. Edward always took care of the paperwork at the ranch, according to Jacke Hendrix Walsh, Frank Jr.'s wife. Jacke moved to the ranch in 1932, when she and Frank Jr. married. They were married in the Walsh Ranch Chapel, a room in the home Frank had built for Concepción. "There was never a question where we would live," she said. "Papa (Frank Sr.) said we could have a room in the house, and that's where we lived. Papa ran things." Her impression of life on the ranch was idyllic. "Mammy (Mrs. Walsh) supervised the kitchen and had a Chinese man and Uncle Burl helping her, the boys (Harry and Edward) had rooms upstairs, Frank and I had our room at

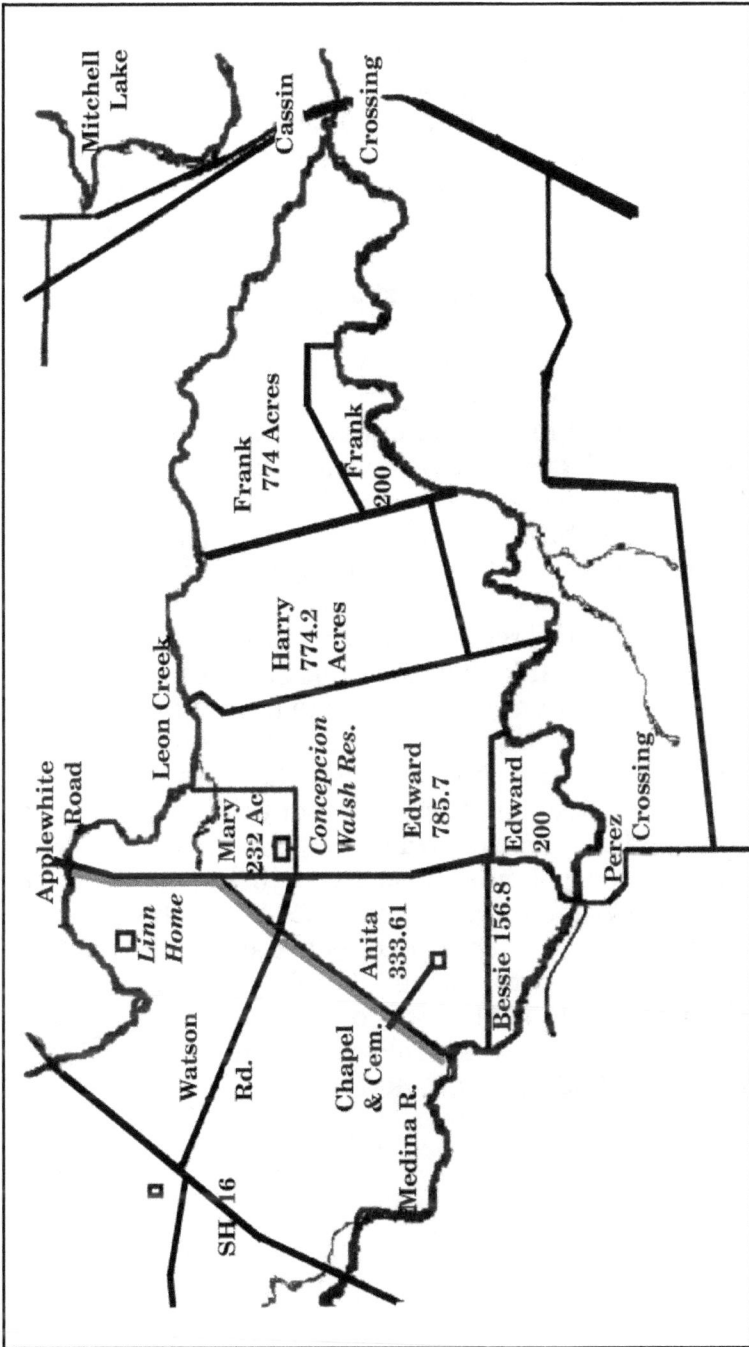

Mitchell Lake

Cassin Crossing

Frank 774 Acres

Frank 200

Harry 774.2 Acres

Leon Creek

Applewhite Road

Mary 232 Ac

Concepcion Walsh Res.

Edward 785.7

Edward 200

Perez Crossing

Linn Home

Watson Rd.

Anita 333.61

Bessie 156.8

Chapel & Cem.

Medina R.

SH 16

Map of ranch showing division of property in 1970s.

the front of the house opening to the big porch. We all lived like one big family." Frank Jr. died in 1981, and Jacke continued to live at the ranch until 1992.

Frank Sr. became ill in the 1930s and was bedfast at the ranch most of the time. During his long illness Frank was attended by a young and pretty registered nurse, Mary Louise Yarborough. Mary Louise was the daughter of a distinguished Louisiana family. After Frank's death in early 1939, Ed, the youngest son, proposed to his dad's nurse and they were married June 10, 1939, in the Walsh Ranch Chapel. The old chapel, where Jose Pérez and others were buried, was already in ruins. Since Frank and Concepción established the chapel in their home, nearly all family marriages were performed there.

By consensus agreement, Edward became ranch manager as his brothers grew older and held the family estate, now divided between six offspring, as one working ranch.

A sister, Lottie, requested her share of the land after marrying W. A. Mahla. Not wanting to split up the ranch, her parents bought adjacent acreage north of Leon Creek and gave it to her with the stipulation she would not receive any of the ranch property. For that reason she is not shown on the division of property set aside in the estates of Frank and Concepción Walsh.

Ed and Mary Louise also lived in the ranch house until their first daughter was born. Ed built a home on his homestead acreage. They had two daughters, Caroline and Patricia Elizabeth Concepción Walsh. The girls were the sixth generation with roots on the ranch. Both attended private schools in San Antonio, graduating from high school at Our Lady of the Lake.

Chapter Seven

The Applewhite Reservoir

Prior to 1974, few people familiar with the Walsh Ranch, as it became known, would have imagined it being a focus of political controversy. That year, 1974, part of the ranch, the scenic and rich bottom-land down by the Medina River, was targeted for a reservoir. The Applewhite Reservoir, to be named after the Linns' former neighbors south of the Medina,[32] was needed to provide an alternate water source, according to the City Water Board (CWB). The reservoir would claim land up to 550 feet mean sea level (MSL) along the Medina basin.

Ed Walsh, representing his brothers and sisters, fought the city bureaucracy to keep the land. Their battle against the Applewhite Reservoir made news in 1974 when the late Paul Thompson, a columnist for the *San Antonio Express-News,* devoted a column to the fight brewing between the Walshes and the CWB over the land. Ed, as spokesman for the family, told the CWB the land was not for sale at any price. He was adamant—the land was their heritage—and he fought the city at every turn, hiring the law firm of Clemens, Weiss, Spencer, and Welmaker to stop the Applewhite fiasco. Other lawyers working for the Walsh family were John Daniels of San Antonio and the firm of Powers and Rose in Austin. Ed's generation literally fought the San Antonio water board to their death beds.

Entering the fray in 1981 was a charismatic young city councilman who had just won the mayoral race, Henry

*The Walsh brothers shown with
Commissioner of Agriculture John White.*

Cisneros. Henry's new role in the movement to use the
Medina River as a water source began to take shape shortly after his election. Before becoming mayor, Cisneros
had carefully avoided issues relating to the city's primary
water source, the Edwards Aquifer. While a councilman,
his predominantly Hispanic constituency had not wanted
anyone tampering with their primary water source. As a
matter of record, Councilman Cisneros and Council-
woman Helen Dutmer told reporters and the council that
". . . the reservoir might resemble a giant mud hole because it will have so little water."[33] Whether it was payback
time for financial backers in the mayoral race, or a mis-

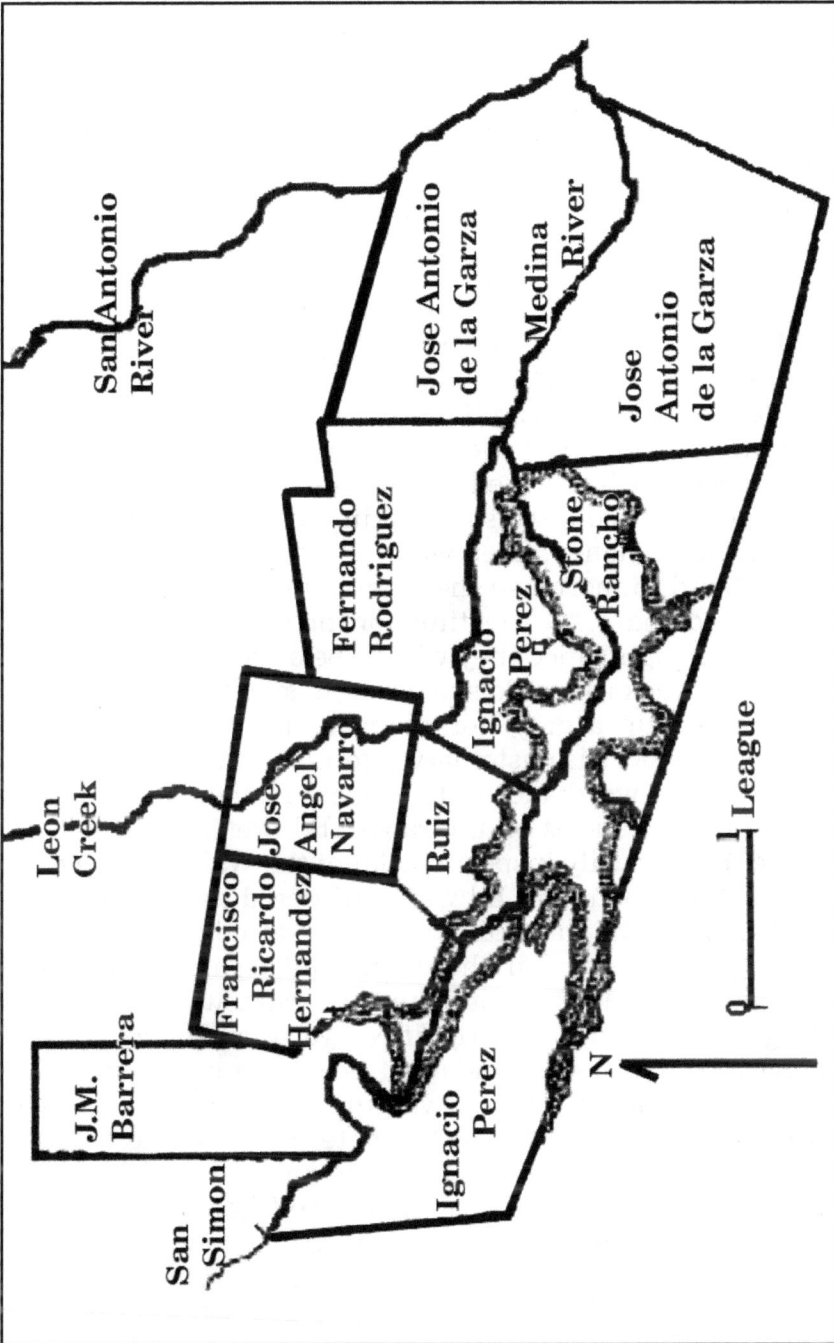

Proposed floodplain of Applewhite reservoir overlaid on map of early ranches on the Medina.

guided effort to solve an age-old concern about surface water, Cisneros galvanized the council to take action on the Applewhite Reservoir almost immediately after taking office.

Ed Walsh had been fighting this battle for a long time and prepared for another skirmish. Lawyers on both sides of the issue prospered. The city legal staff brought in private law firms to help their case at considerable cost to taxpayers.

Legal fees cut deeply into the Walsh family's savings with little success by their highly paid lawyers. Shortly before Ed's accidental death, he could no longer afford the legal battle and told the other family members it was time to give up. They were "land rich" but "cash poor." Their lawyers had asked for another $15,000, which Ed did not have, and he was not asking his sisters and brothers for more money. Even when his daughter and son-in-law offered to mortgage their home for the extra money, Ed was adamant, ". . . it's time for the rest of San Antonio to join the fight since they will all be affected."

Only weeks after Ed's decision to stop the legal battle he saddled up a gray horse, given him by his brother Harry, to make his customary afternoon ride through the pastures and woodlands of the ranch. Despite a variety of off-the-road vehicles on the ranch, Ed preferred to ride a horse for this daily inspection. All of the Walsh men were expert horsemen, and Ed was considered the best of the lot. The horse he was riding had been raised on the ranch. As Ed put his left foot in the stirrup and began to swing his right leg over the horse, it bolted and ran toward the nearest gate, dragging Ed nearly fifteen yards and cracking his pelvis. Ed told his son-in-law of hearing a noise, like the crack of a rifle, as he was swinging up on the horse. The frightened horse halted at the gate. Ed was able to disentangle his left foot from the stirrup and pull himself back toward the barn, propping himself against the fence and calling for help. John Small, his son-in-law, found him there several hours later, and Ed was rushed to a hospital where he died a few weeks later from internal injuries.

With this bastion of resistance gone, it did not take the CWB and City Council long to purge board members opposed to Applewhite. The council, led by Mayor Cisneros, moved quickly to approve Applewhite, a half-billion dollar project that many who lived along the Medina said would literally never hold water. Ironically, most of the real estate needed for the project once belonged to Ignacio Pérez. The Applewhite project included a dam across the Medina River, a diversion channel from Leon Creek to the Medina, a water purification plant, and city-wide distribution mains.

The CWB's final offer to the Walsh and Small families for their 590 acres along the Medina amounted to nearly $2.7 million ($2.32 million original offer and $370,000 in extra payments to withdraw a lawsuit). In south Bexar County $4,500 an acre for ranch land is a good price. But, when one factors in access lost to working oil wells and oil reserves (no estimate is available on the value of the oil reserves), and access lost to water and bottom land grazing for their cattle, the family's bottom line was marginal. Furthermore, gravel deposits worth hundreds of thousands of dollars lie beneath the condemned land bought by the CWB. Estimates by a geologist suggest there is more than $500,000 in gravel alone.

Perhaps to help the cause of surface water (and increase the need for an alternative water source), a catfish farmer named Ronnie Pucek was allowed to drill a well deep into the Edwards Aquifer near the Medina River. The resulting artesian gusher made headlines across the state and was the subject of an article in the October 1991 issue of *Texas Monthly*. Water flowing from the catfish farmer's well ranged from one-quarter to one-half the daily usage of water by all of the CWB's customers. The used water ran about two hundred yards down a tree-lined, gravel-bottomed draw into the Medina River. Land where the catfish farm was developed once belonged to Don Juan Ignacio Pérez de Casanova. The "old colonel" had walked the land and claimed it in 1808, paid taxes on it and used it until his death. His son lost that portion of the *rancho* to "new Texans" in 1836, as previously mentioned.

Artesian well at Living Waters Catfish Farm. Control valves on the free-flowing well have long since been closed.

Water spewing from the giant pipe had a sulfuric (rotten egg) smell. An explanation offered was that this water was coming from the bottom of the Edwards Aquifer at a depth of perhaps 200-300 feet below MSL where the water was of poor quality. The vacuum caused as water was being drawn from the bottom of the aquifer sucked more of San Antonio's good drinking water down into the less desirable area. Not to worry, said business leaders and political figures. They assured the public that Lake Applewhite would give San Antonio a source of quality drinking water and reduce dependence on the aquifer. While saying this in public, they were privately pushing their development projects over the aquifer recharge zone.

As water from the catfish farm met the Medina River,

Medina River flowing past Pérez Crossing at Applewhite Road during the time catfish farm was in operation.

river levels and rate of flow increased downstream at Pérez Crossing on Applewhite Road. River water rushing past the crossing smelled of the same "rotten egg" odor permeating the area around the artesian well on the catfish farm. It also took on a leaden look. Apparently CWB planners and the city staff had been counting on water from "Living Waters Catfish Farm" to fill the reservoir.

The economics of drilling a deep well to provide water for a catfish farm, constructing concrete tanks with automated feeders, and doing this in a drought prone area, boggles the mind. There had to be another reason, and Pucek revealed it later in defending the project. Not only did he plan to operate the catfish farm, but he wanted to sell the water he was pumping into the Medina, via his catfish tanks, to the highest bidder.

Exploring the area condemned for Applewhite, a gaping crevice that began as a small crack in the soil surface got progressively deeper and wider as it stretched toward the land cleared for the Applewhite Dam. It seemed evident that even with the flow from the huge well, crevices such as this would suck water from the reservoir faster than it could fill. Perhaps that is why long-term residents had said earlier the lake would not hold water. The state has since forced Pucek to shutoff his well at "Living Waters Catfish Farm" and the river flow returned to normal.

The remaining family members resigned themselves to the loss of land and reached an agreement with the city in the spring of 1991, before a citywide vote was to take place on the Applewhite issue. Although construction had already begun and surveys made, the property owners were not paid until December 1991, their money held in escrow during that time. Ironically, citizens of San Antonio rejected the 45,250-acre feet Applewhite Reservoir (at 536 feet MSL) and water treatment plant as a waste of taxpayer dollars. The giant pecan, cypress, and oak trees on Walsh Ranch would have soon fallen to bulldozers if voters had not brought a halt to the project.

The people who voted down the Applewhite project halted dissection of the oldest working ranch in Texas. In 1975 the Texas Family Land Heritage Program recognized the Walsh-Pérez Ranch on Applewhite Road as the oldest ranch/farm in Texas owned and operated continuously by the same family. It may be the oldest in North America still owned and operated by the same family. (See endnote 1.) That may be worth a roadside marker one of these days.

Chapter Eight

The Seventh Generation

Patricia Elizabeth Concepción Walsh, previously mentioned as a sixth generation descendant of the "old colonel," married John Hart Small, son of the late James William and Constance Small, in 1973. John, an accountant and St. Mary's University graduate, had operated his parents' farm in south Bexar County and was familiar with the cattle business. Patricia was a graduate of St. Mary's University, had a master's degree from Our Lady of the Lake, and a doctorate in education from Texas A&M. She has always had an interest in the Spanish history of the ranch. The Smalls raised their three children, John Edward, Patrick, and Elizabeth (the seventh generation of Pérez descendants to have lived on the ranch) to be a part of the ranch heritage. They have experienced the cattle roundups, harvesting the crops, cookouts by the river, and hunted the land.

Patricia's careful retelling of the family oral history has benefited several writers. She is now an assistant principal in the Harlandale School District. John is a retired accountant, and formerly headed the city audit department. Before Applewhite was a done deal, John and Patricia purchased several hundred acres of the original grant from one of Patricia's aunts who wanted to sell within the family. A son, Patrick, was deeded fifty acres of land and oil royalties by his great-uncle Harry in 1984. A significant portion of the land owned by Bessie, Anita, Edward, and Harry Walsh (and/or heirs of) was con-

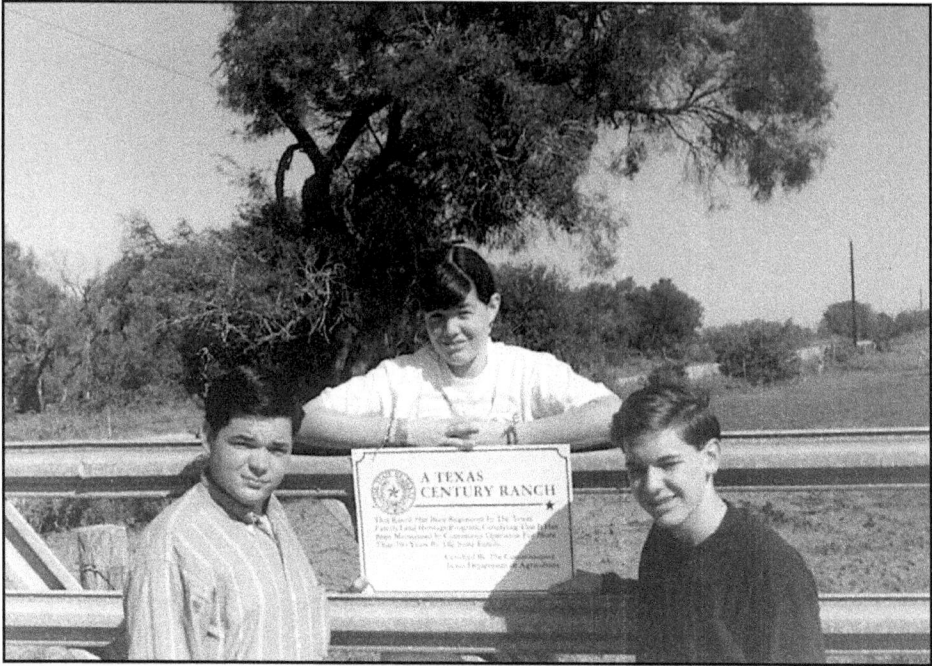

The Seventh Generation—John Edward, Elizabeth, and Patrick Small pose at the entry gate to their part of the ranch. The sign designates the ranch as "A Texas Century Ranch." Photograph taken in 1990.

demned for Applewhite. However, the heirs of Bessie and Anita retained possession of their property as the Applewhite project was eventually canceled and they had not been paid.

After her father's death, Patricia and John Small worked with the CWB trying to salvage as much as they could of the historic ranch from the grasp of Applewhite. They moved out to the ranch to maintain their herd of cattle and to help Patricia's mother run her portion of the ranch.

Sharing her father's love of the ranch and its history, it saddened Patricia to see sections of the original ranch sold outside the family. From well over 20,000 acres in the

South side of early Walsh Ranch Chapel. Grave sites are to the left and some burials have taken place inside the chapel.

early 1800s, the ranch was reduced to 4,000 plus acres in 1851, and has now dwindled to slightly more than 2,000 acres in family hands. Some of that land is leased outside the family.

Ed Walsh was having the original chapel restored before his death. Only exterior walls had been repaired. The grave sites were in a state of neglect. (See photo.) Those buried in the cemetery include Jose Ignacio Pérez (1786-1852); his wife, Maria Josefa Cortinas Pérez (1786-1861); their son-in-law, Jacob Linn (1825-1878); Jacob's wife, Maria Josefa de Jesus de Anastacia Toribia Pérez Linn (1824-1889); and Ignacio del Refugio Pérez, Ignacio Martin Pérez, and Maria Trinidad Pérez, all children of Jose Ignacio and his wife. Recently Frances Walsh Mahla Gembler, daughter of Lottie Walsh Mahla, was buried in the abandoned chapel of the cemetery at her request.

Had Ed Walsh lived through the Applewhite debacle and maintained the physical integrity of the ranch, the differences that now exist between family members might never have occurred. Ongoing legal issues between sixth generation descendants of Pérez may make family ranching a little more difficult. "But," as one family member put it, "our family has survived a lot of hardships, revolutions, Indians, squatters, and droughts. A legal squabble isn't going to keep us from ranching."

To cap the historical significance of the ranch, an archeological "dig" required for the Applewhite project found Indian artifacts dating from 6000 BC. Artifacts and fossils found by University of Texas San Antonio (UTSA) archeologist Al McGraw received little publicity during the election campaign in 1991.

This ranch, dotted with fragments of history, and blessed with a great variety of vegetation and trees found along the Medina and other rivers throughout South Texas, was being preserved by the family as a working ranch. Generations of family members fought Indians, land grabbers, and bureaucracies to keep it, only to lose the most cherished portion to the City of San Antonio for a reservoir that will never be built.

For more than 200 years the Pérez-Linn-Walsh-Small families raised crops, cattle, and horses on their land. The voters' reprieve gave the Walsh and Small families a few more years to ranch on a scale that is profitable, and to enjoy the beauty of the river bottoms. The loss of the river bottom land has effectively limited the numbers of cattle that can be maintained on the remaining acreage. And, in so doing, may have cut off the only chance this historic ranch has to survive (as a ranch) in today's cattle market. The city leased the land back to the Walsh and Small families to use in their cattle operations while SAWS attempts to define a useful purpose for their land along the Medina.

During 1997, John Edward Small was kind enough to guide some visitors over what remains of the ranch. There were a few cattle to be seen in the pastures (the main herd was being pastured at Elmendorf) and evidence of wild

A team of Texas A&M University geologists were staking survey points in the Medina bottoms of the old Pérez ranch in the spring of 1997. John Edward, on the right, greeted the team.

turkey, feral hogs, and deer hunters. They even ran across some Texas A&M University archeologists digging and setting markers for aerial mapping of the historic sites. Perry Roehl, a San Antonio geologist, was impressed by the exposed geological formations on the ranch. "An unexpected find in this part of Bexar County," he commented.

In 1998, the SAWS board began listening to recommendations from civic groups on what should be done with the 2,400 acres condemned for the Applewhite Reservoir. The acreage taken from the Walsh-Small families will remain part of that package and be used for whatever purposes the city owned utility determines. It would be fitting if someone remembers the family that had the

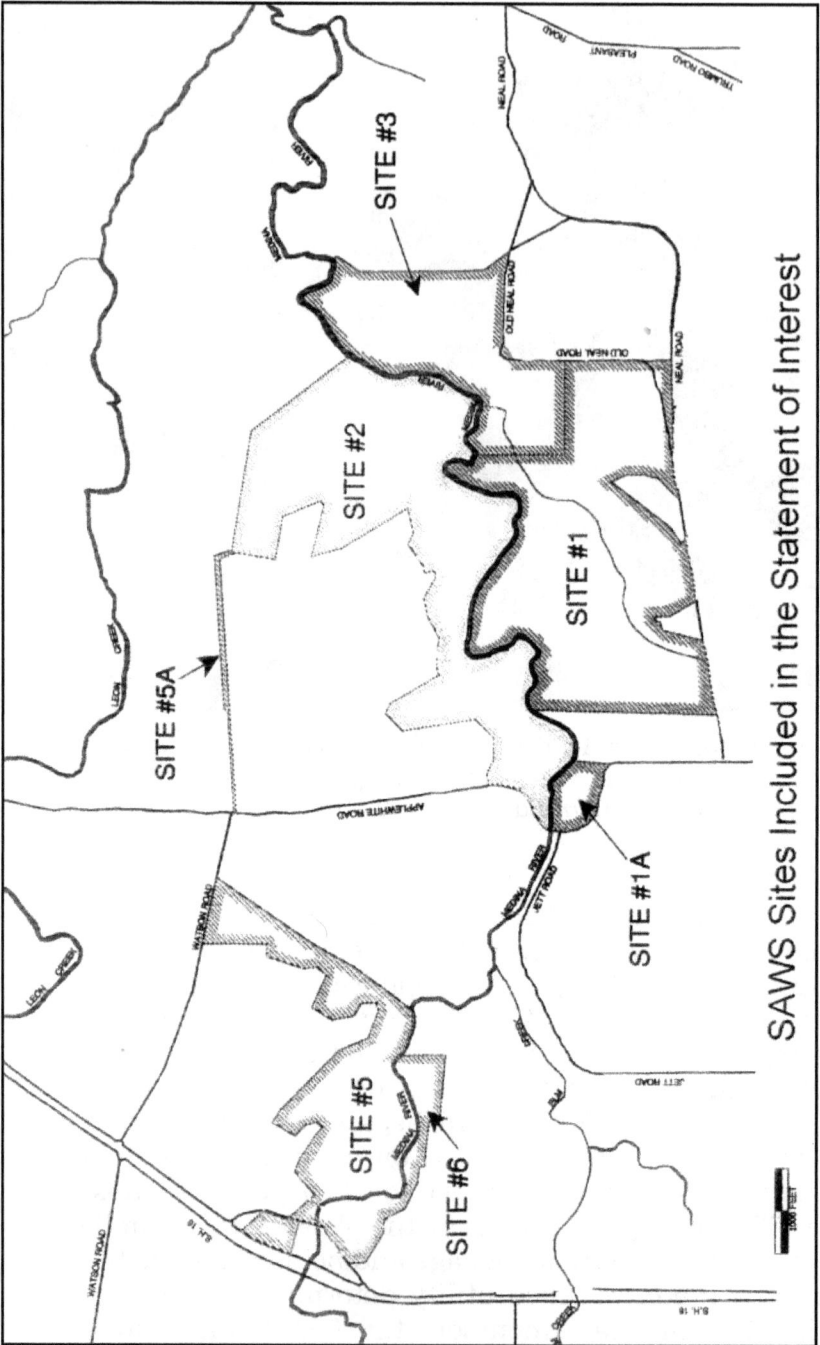

SAWS Sites Included in the Statement of Interest

Texas A&M has proposed using several sites owned by SAWS for a "Land Heritage Institute." Site #2 is on the old Pérez ranch and would be used as an example of a Spanish Colonial cattle operation.

Pérez brand.

most to lose, and the oldest ranch in Texas, when that determination is made.

A proposal from Texas A&M to use the land as a "Land Heritage Institute of the Americas" is being studied by SAWS. If adopted the Walsh land north of the Medina would be developed as a "Spanish Colonial cattle-grazing operation typical of the late 1700s and early 1800s." SAWS land opposite the Walsh-Small Ranch, on the south bank of the Medina, would be turned into an Antebellum and Tenant Farm exhibit, and a Native American section to include a farm of the future.

Meanwhile, John Edward, host of the 1997 visit, lives in his granddad's ranch house, checks the fences, tends the cattle, drives the tractor, bales the hay, and is an outgoing, gregarious escort to those who visit the oldest ranch in Texas. And, when he is not busy, he attends classes at Palo Alto College and UTSA, taking business and agriculture courses. His younger brother, Patrick, is majoring in history at UTSA and plans to attend law school upon graduation. Elizabeth is a junior at UTSA majoring in marketing. All three of these young people have cattle on the land. Patrick Small recently registered the original brand of Juan Ygnacio Pérez to use on their cattle. If one looks closely at the brand the vertical J and P are apparent, and the horizontal Y is skillfully inserted at the mid-section.

What SAWS decides may determine the fate of the oldest ranch in Texas. Whether it gets swallowed up by a rapidly growing city, is turned into a regional heritage center, or is allowed to continue as a historically significant operating ranch is yet to be determined. If the seventh generation of Pérez descendants is the last to ranch on this land, they have determined not to give in easily. No other family has stuck to their land as they have. One generation passes away, another comes, but the land is forever.

Appendices

APPENDIX A

CAMPAIGN AGAINST THE LIPANES

1798

Note: "The manuscript from which this narrative was taken is deposited in the Library of the University of Texas. A copy is in the vaults of the County Clerk of Bexar County, Albert Trawalter. The principal witness concerning the raids committed by the Comanches and Apaches was Ygnacio Pérez, who was supposedly the owner of the Governor's Palace, and after having been *alcalde* of San Antonio for a few years, became acting governor of Texas in 1817."

(The copy from which this was taken is in the San Antonio Public Library.)

Misc. 64-7613.

I went to the home of Ygnacio Pérez, whom I have known through many circumstances, and after cautiously informing him that I had a matter to discuss with him in private, I promised him on my honor as a man, that I would consider everything confidential.

When we were in private, I asked him, "What damages have been wrought by the Allied Indians of this Presidio and its ranches to its residents and their properties?"

He replied that he knew that the Indians, who under the name of "Allies," frequently visit this Presidio, where they are given gifts, and here celebrate their campaign, they say, against the Lipanes. After leaving the Presidio loaded with gifts (en route to their settlements), they steal every horse that is unfettered and even those belonging to the ranchers, which they find during their slaughtering raids and round-up of wild horses.

He also declared that those assigned to the raids work down the river, raiding the ranches situated there, and that, in addition to these robberies, the said Indians cause other damages, such as the slaughter of beef cattle and the destruction of the property of the settler, whom they ill-treat and abuse personally when the settlers attempt to stop such slaughter. Pérez added that on one occasion in January or February 1795, while he was in company with seven other neighbors on the banks of the San Marcos, the Comanche Indians came to the place where they were making ox-carts, and stole two horses. He declared that he decided to follow them with some of his own men. On reaching their settlement, he found two Indians with one of the stolen horses, which Pérez and his men immediately recaptured, but soon eight more Comanches arrived and immediately began to curse the Spaniards, finally firing at them and wounding the speaker (Pérez) in the left, I mean right, shoulder. Pérez and his men immediately returned fire, whereupon the Indians, after one had been wounded, pleaded for peace, which was granted on condition that they give a gun as compensation for the missing horse, which, no doubt, had been spirited away by the horse thief. This they did, and the Indians departed, leaving this narrator to work on his *carretas*.

Asked if he knew of other damages done by the Comanches or other Indians, he replied that every time they crossed they robbed the corn-fields and vegetable gardens, even those adjacent to the houses of the Presidio.

Pérez declared that it was well and notoriously known that the Indians from the Nation of the Tancahues recently assaulted the citizen Bernardo Cervantes because he tried to protect his crops, and they committed worse outrages at the ranch of Joaquin Leal, for, after having destroyed his crops, they attempted to attack his wife and another woman living there, but these women, pretending to fetch water for the Tancahues, fled under cover of the darkness to another ranch, carrying their children with them, and thus escaped.

The Indians carried away all they could find, such as powder, bullets, and whatever else was lying around.

Asked if he knew at what time this happened, he replied that he did not remember the day, but it was in the month of July 1797.

He was questioned as to whether he knew of other damages done by the aforesaid Indians, and if so to please state them clearly as it was important information; he replied that there were so many that it was not possible to remember them in detail, or to describe them correctly, as they were daily occurrence.

Among the most recent outrages was a raid committed before the very eyes of the owners, the theft and removal of many head of cows, goats, and ewes, and their slaughter, which took place at the ranch of Ygnacio Calvillo.

I asked if any measures had been taken to curb, punish, and avenge such hostilities. He replied that he had neither seen any punishment meted out nor even an attempt to prevent these outrages, for, while it was true that soldiers sometimes were dispatched to prevent them, the number of soldiers sent was always so small in proportion to the number of Indians that sometimes they carried on their depredations even before the eyes of the soldiers. Furthermore, while a small body of soldiers was ordered to escort a priest who was going to Nacogdoches, they were attacked by a body of Tancahues who seized all their horses, packs, baggage, and everything they had and were carrying to that town.

Asked if said Indians had ever returned the horses, baggage, etc., he replied that several Indians had returned some horses, together with twenty to thirty pesos in cash, and some books of the said priest, but Perez could not state in detail just which articles were recovered.

Asked if he knew that the Governor had refused to render assistance when requested by the settlers, and if he could give dates and names of persons, he replied that, while not alleging it as a positive fact, it was generally known that such assistance has been reluctantly given by the said Governor, often with harsh resentful words spoken to the person requesting his aid, and that this aid has been so pitifully small that the settlers have recovered little of their losses, and they have been unable to prevent further damages.

Asked if he knew how many soldiers were assigned to guard the horses and how many there were to date, he replied that formerly there were thirty men on guard, but only twenty-five now.

Asked how many herds of horses and mares of the citizens remained after they were separated from those of the soldiers, he replied that when such division was made there were, besides a few herds of colts, about 800 gentle horses, but today there are scarcely 500.

Asked why all herds were not grazed together or near each other, he replied that the army horses were moved constantly for reasons unknown to him, and the others were kept where the grazing was best.

Asked if he knew who had killed a Tancahue Indian near the Presidio, and if he knew whether or not Spaniards living in this city or elsewhere had stolen horses, crops or had slaughtered cattle belonging to other owners, he replied that, regarding the Indian of the Tancahue Nation, he had died in the Municipality of San Antonio de Valero, and it was known that he was killed by the Lipanes, led by Chambalia; concerning the robberies and killing of cattle, these were committed by some bad Christians, fugitives, and thieves at different times, but after investigations were made the guilty ones were punished; this was all he could reply to the questions he had been asked. He signed this declaration in San Antonio de Bexar and this Presidio, January 24, 1798.

Andres Benito Courbier,   Ygnasio (sic) Perez,
[Rubric]   [Rubric]

APPENDIX B

WILL OF JUAN YGNACIO PEREZ

As Lieutenant Colonel Don Ygnacio Perez wishes to make his will, I commission you to draw up and execute this document with Don Francisco Collantes, Second Lieutenant of the Militia, acting as Secretary. You will compose said document according to the form prescribed by the royal orders, transmitting it to the government for its due effect; and certified copies will be given to the parties who request them. I hope you will not delay a moment in performing this duty I have assigned to you because of the critical condition of the patient. May God keep you many years.

Bexar, June 16, 1820. Antonio Martinez. To the Honorable Captain Don Juan de Castañeda

By virtue of the preceding order under today's date, I, Don Juan de Castañeda, have been commissioned by the Honorable Governor of this Province, Colonel Antonio Martinez, to draw up the will of Lieutenant Colonel Don Ygnacio Pérez, and as the same Honorable Governor has appointed the Second Lieutenant of Militia, Don Francisco Collantes, as Secretary, he was required to take the respective oath. On doing so he promised on his word of honor to act in secrecy and good faith and to operate with complete legality at all times, and in evidence thereof he signed with me in the city of San Fernando de Bexar on July 16, 1820.

Immediately on the same day of said month and year, the honorable Captain, Don Juan de Castañeda, to begin the formation of the will of the Honorable Lieutenant Colonel Don Ygnacio Pérez, ordered the citation of Don Luis Galan, Don Jose Antonio Saucedo, Don Manuel Barrera, and the Parish Priest who is serving as military chaplain of this city, and having been asked and summoned by the party to be present as instrumental witnesses on the same day at the dwelling of said Honorable Lieutenant Colonel, I, the undersigned Notary so notified and informed them, placing it of record which said Honorable Judge signed; I certify.

Juan de Castañeda   Juan Francisco de Collantes

In the city of San Fernando de Bexar on the same day of said month and year, I, Captain Don Juan de Castañeda, accompanied by the Notary and instrumental witnesses, went to the dwelling of Lieutenant Colonel Don Ygnacio Pérez who was ill, and all being present and the patient being in full possession of his faculties, I instructed him to proceed with making his last will and testament, and so informed he began to do so in the following terms: In the name of God, Our all powerful Lord, and to his honor and glory let it be clearly known and evident to those who shall see the present instrument that I, Don Ygnacio Pérez, legitimate son of Don Domingo Perez and Dona Concepcion Carvajal, now deceased, a native of this city of Bexar, baptized in the parish church of the same city, of married status, and fifty-nine years of age, although being ill and confined to my bed by chance occurrences which God, our Lord, has seen fit to permit, do give Him infinite thanks for preserving me with a completely sound mind, believing, as I do believe, in the deep and incomprehensible Mystery and one single Divine Being, in the incarnation of the Divine Word, Christ born of the Virgin Mary, Our Most Holy Lady, in the Most Holy Sacrament of the Altar, and in all the other mysteries and sacraments which our Holy Mother Church, the Apostolic Roman Catholic, believes, teaches, predicates, and defends, under which faith and belief I have lived and expect to die as a faithful Catholic and Christian, in order that the hour of my death will not find me unprepared in regard to a clear conscience. By the present instrument and in the most sufficient form of the law, I declare the following:

I commit my soul to God, our Lord, who created me from nothing, and I consign my body to the earth from which it came, and once it becomes a corpse, I order it covered with the habit of our Father San Francisco and buried in the parish church of this city with the ceremony of High Mass and a watch over the present body, all the priests being in attendance and for the salvation of my soul, a Novena of High Masses.

Article. I wish to leave twenty-five pesos to the widows and orphans of those who have died in the present war, as disposed by royal order, and also all the customary forced legacies.

Article. I declare that I am united in holy matrimony with Doña Clemencia Hernandez, from which marriage we have descendants, and we recognize as our legitimate children Don

Jose Ygnacio, Doña Maria Gertrudis, and Doña Concepción, whom I designate as my legitimate and universal heirs.

Article. I declare that when I married my said wife neither she nor I had any capital and that we have acquired our property and household items by our own personal labor, and in particular by that of my wife.

Article. I declare as my property my dwelling which is composed of the lodgings adjacent to the house of Don Jose Flores and extending up the corner of Calle del Fuerte and back to the creek, situated on the Plaza de Armas; another situated on the street or opposite the house of Don Francisco Flores, and adjacent to it three lodgings constructed of wood, and others already begun, with wood and stone for their construction; and also another house on the street of Don Manuel Barrera to the north, and a stone lodging on the street of Don Jose Antonio Saucedo.

Article. I declare that I have five days of water and the corresponding amount of irrigable in the Lower Labor Field, and between said days there are five hours of water which belong to the relatives of my wife who also has an interest in said hours of water.

Article. I declare that I have a ranch of four leagues for large stock on the other side of the Medina River and another league on this side donated to me by the Honorable Commandant General of the Western Provinces, Don Nemesio Salcedo, for my services; on this league there is a stone house and wooden corrals which I own in good faith and by order of said Commandant General, the title to which should exist in the Archives of this Government. On these pasture lands there is some large stock both branded and unbranded, which I consider part of my property.

Article. I declare that I have twenty-three mules with harness of knotted rope and fifteen mules with trace chains, and all the horses and mules marked with my brand after my son Jose Ygnacio has taken those he chooses as his since he acquired them by his own personal labor and industry, and not having a brand, he used mine.

Article. I declare that in the possession of Don Xayme Garza, Chief Adjutant and Surgeon of the Army and resident of Monclova, I have three thousand pesos in cash, and I also have two thousand pesos in the possession of the Honorable Archdeacon of the Holy Cathedral Church of Monterrey, Don Juan

Ysidro Campos; also two thousand three hundred and forty-three in the possession of Captain Don Rafael Gonzales, to be collected for amounts supplied to this Government for the companies; also two thousand pesos in cash in possession of my wife. I also have farming equipment, oxen, and other movable goods connected with this business, of which my wife has knowledge. Also I leave all the advances I have earned during the time I have served our Sovereign, according to the adjustments made by the respective paymasters.

Article. I declare that I have a slave called Salvador whom I bought for four hundred pesos, and it is my wish that he be valued at two hundred pesos, as my aforesaid heirs understand.

Article. I declare that Don Yrineo Castellon owes me one hundred pesos in silver which I lent him, and from this amount twenty-five pesos is to be deducted as I have a mule of his, and if he does not agree to this, he can settle the matter with my executors.

Article. It is my wish that my executors collect all amounts the companies and other individuals owe me, as shown by documents in my possession; also that they pay all my debts, those under my signature or any legal bills presented against me.

Article. I declare that besides the five days of water referred to I have twelve additional hours in said Labor. Two of these are in controversy with Don Francisco Flores, which my executors will settle; if said Flores proves they are his, they will deliver them to him, and they will give four of the remaining ten to my servant Manuel Quintero for his loyalty and service.

Article. It is my wish that one hundred pesos be taken from my "third" and "fifth" parts of the estate and divided among my poorest relatives, and I have so informed my wife.

Article. I declare that all the useful household furniture, ornaments, clothes, and jewelry is to be given to my wife as dowry.

Article. I declare that I wish the best of my horses, arms, saddle trappings, and ordinary clothing given to my grandchild Don Jose Ygnacio Perez.

Article. I declare that I wish to increase the share of my son Don Jose Ygnacio in the "third" and "fifth" parts of my estate by deducting from the overall amount of my wealth the cost of my funeral, burial, and forced legacies, and from said increase will be taken the one hundred pesos mentioned in Article 13, which will be covered by the stock he freely chooses, in consid-

eration of his complete obedience and for his having contributed by his personal labor to the acquisition of the stock, as
I have said and also indicate by this statement.

Article. I declare that in consideration of the loyalty of my
son Jose Ygnacio who has not pursued any special interests
other than the common increase of my estate, it is my wish that
although my dwelling has been already donated by reason of
marriage, and understanding that its total value is twelve hundred pesos at this time, I wish to remunerate him for his said
services, and I hereby bequeath it to him, my wife being in complete agreement, and I order that the donation be considered as
a wedding gift.

Article. I declare that the lodging situated on the street of
Don Jose Antonio Saucedo is to be left to Margarita Richar
whom we adopted as our daughter at the time of her birth fifteen years ago, in order for her to live under the jurisdiction of
our country, my wife and I being in agreement in regard to this
donation.

Article. I declare that the house located on the street of Don
Manuel Barrera, to the north, cost five hundred pesos. My
daughter Concepción has received it as her legitimate inheritance along with three hundred and thirty pesos which I have
supplied in separate transactions, all of which will be taken into
account as the guardianship of a minor. I declare it in evidence
thereof.

Article. I declare that the amounts given to my daughter
Gertrudis after her marriage have been in recompense or remu-
nerative payment of larger amounts or advances which my
aforesaid daughter Gertrudis has made to me and my family.
Therefore, no one will be charged with this. It is my just wish. I
declare it in evidence thereof.

Article. I declare this as my estate, and after payment of the
funeral and burial expenses, forced legacies, and the new tax, it
is my wish that my aforesaid heirs take the part belonging to
me and enjoy it with God's blessing and mine.

Article. I declare that in order to complete this my last will
I appoint as executors and guardians of my estate: first, my wife
Dona Clemencia Hernandez; second, my son-in-law Brigadier
Don Antonio Cordero; third, my legitimate son Don Jose Ygnacio, so that on my death they may take possession of my estate,
sell all that is necessary at public auction, or privately, and from
the returns, complete the transactions and pay whatever is nec-

essary since to each one separately and to all jointly I give full power and authority insofar as the law requires, the first named having preference in all cases.

And by the present I cancel and revoke all wills and testamentary dispositions previously made verbally, in writing, or in any other form so that none will be valid or receive credit in or out of judicature, except this will and memorial which I desire and order to be considered and honored as such and as my last deliberative disposition in the best legal form. I execute and sign it in the foresaid city on the same day of said month and year, with said Assisting Judge and Priest. Done before me, the present Notary and attendant witnesses, which I certify.

Ygnacio Perez / Juan de Castañeda / Bachelor Refugio de la Garza
Before me, Juan Francisco de Collantes.

(A codicil to the will was made in 1823, with all the attendant appointments and notaries.)

In the city of San Fernando de Bexar on September 3, 1823, I Juan de Castañeda, accompanied by the Secretary, went to the home of the patient, Colonel Ygnacio Pérez, and the Honorable Parish Priest, the witnesses, Don Juan Jose Arocha, and Don Gaspar Flores being present and having indicated to the patient that they were ready to execute his last will, he produced a sealed file of papers said to be his will, dated, July 16, 1820; and having been opened by the Secretary in my presence and that of the appointed witnesses, the will was read in its entirety; and in full possession of his faculties the said colonel took the papers and began to revoke and change some articles of the aforesaid will, thus increasing the real estate acquired subsequent to the former provisions as follows:

Article. I declare that the money which appeared to have been in possession of Don Xayme and my wife, Dona Clemencia, as stated in Article 9, no longer exists since the former has paid that amount and some of it has been invested in various lands and houses, and some has been spent in the negotiation of my affairs. Therefore, only one thousand nine hundred pesos in cash are due me by the will of the late Archdeacon, Don Juan Ysidro Campos, which my executors will collect when convenient, with the understanding that although the debt with said

Mortuary was two thousand pesos, he made a payment of one hundred pesos to my son-in-law, Don Fernando Rodriguez; therefore Article 9 is canceled and is not valid. In regard to the seven thousand pesos in currency which is reduced by one thousand nine hundred pesos, Captain Don Rafael Gonzales is likewise not responsible for the two thousand three hundred and forty-three pesos as stated in Article 9. They were in his possession for collection from the troops, and said Captain has returned them along with other claims of the same kind, and they remain in possession of my wife.

Article. I declare that according to various entries which appear in the memorandum I have kept, I have furnished my son-in-law Don Fernando Rodriguez and my daughter Doña Concepcion, his wife the amount of one thousand six hundred and eight pesos, and it is the duty of my executors to determine what part corresponds to my daughter Concepción as her guardianship.

Article. I declare that of the two thousand pesos which I lent to my late son-in-law, Brigadier Don Antonio Cordero, which by natural oversight I did not mention in my former statement, he sent to me by conduct of my daughter Gertrudis, his wife, the receipts which appear in the account I have kept, and they amount to five hundred and seventy-five pesos; and having subtracted these from the former amount, one thousand four hundred and twenty-five are yet due from my said son-in-law, but with respect to the service rendered to my daughter and her husband not having left anything with which to pay them, it is my wish to which she fully consents, that for payment they be included and discounted as her corresponding guardianship, and I charge my executors to do so as a last favor in my last will.

Article. I declare that my said daughter Gertrudis owes me five hundred and fifteen pesos, seven reales, the rest of nine hundred and seventy-seven pesos which I lent her in Real de Cuencame when she was returning from Durango to this city for her widow's pension. My executors will present this amount for discount as her corresponding guardianship.

Article. I declare that in order to fulfill my last and final will with respect to the death of the second executor, my son-in-law Brigadier Don Antonio Cordero, who was appointed in my foregoing testament, I name as executors and administrators of this my last and final testament, first, my wife Dona Clemencia

Hernandez, second, my son, Don Jose Ygnacio, and third, Don Domingo Bustillos of this community, so that on my death they may take possession of my estate, sell what is necessary from the best of it at public auction or otherwise, as may be most convenient, and from the proceeds do everything that needs to be done since to each one separately and to all jointly I give full power and authority insofar as the law requires, and in all cases the first named executor shall have preference.

And by the present I annul and revoke all wills and other testamentary dispositions I have made previously (excepting the present) in written, verbal, or any other form so that they may never be valid or given credit in or out of judicature. I wish and order that this codicil be considered my last deliberative disposition in due legal form. He so granted and signed in the aforesaid city on the same day of said month and year with said Judge attended by the aforesaid Honorable Priest, before me, the present Secretary and afore-mentioned instrumental witnesses, which I certify. Ygnacio Perez. Juan de Castañeda. Bachelor Francisco Maynes. Secretary, Juan Tiburcio de Castañeda.

(Virginia H. Taylor made this translation of the will of Ygnacio Perez from a copy recorded in the Bexar County Clerk's office. Parts of perfunctory statements have been omitted.—Author.)

Glossary

Acequia: Irrigation canal, or ditch.

Alamo: Poplar or cottonwood tree. Valero Mission in early San Antonio is now called the Alamo.

Alcalde: Mayor, or justice of peace.

Bexar: Pronounced bay-har (Spanish) or bay-er, is a name commonly applied to Presidio of San Antonio de Béjar and the Villa San Fernando de Béjar. It is now the name of the county in which San Antonio is found.

Cabildo: A cathedral chapter, or municipal council.

Casa: A house, home, or household.

Compañía Volante: Literally a flying company, used to describe a mounted cavalry unit.

Despoblado: An uninhabited, desolate place.

Don: Title accorded to men entering first level of Spanish nobility.

Doña: Title conferred on women of Spanish nobility.

El Camino Real: The Royal Road, or the major road.

Jacale: An adobe hut, or shack.

Labor or labore: About 177 acres of land. A forerunner of the family-sized farm.

League: A unit of distance equal to three statute miles, or 2.63 nautical miles.

Manadas: Herds or droves. Usually referring to horses.

Nueva España: New Spain.

Pobladores: Settlers.

Presidio: A garrison, or fortress, established by the Spanish to protect their holdings and missions.

Rancho: A place where cattle, horses, sheep, and/or goats are raised for resale.

Rancho de la Purísima Concepción: Ranch named in honor of Concepción Mission.

91

San Antonio de Béjar: San Antonio and its environs. Sometimes called San Fernando de Béjar, or Bexar.

Sindico de Ranchos: Person in charge of ranches in a region.

Sitio: A square league of land equivalent to 4,428 acres.

Vamos alla: Let's go there.

Vara: Approximately one yard (33 1/3 inches).

Endnotes

1. Spanish land grants in Florida were voided in the 1800s and the historic ranches of three Spanish soldiers in California, circa 1784, have been swallowed by Los Angeles and San Diego. The Arizona Historical Society has no record of Spanish grant ranches still in existence and New Mexico grants of the 1700s were bought out by investors in the late 1800s. Mexican land reforms during the century of enlightenment, the eighteenth century, and the scarcity of surviving documents from earlier periods, lead one to believe an older *rancho* does not exist.

2. Bexar Archives, July 18, 1795.

3. Bexar Archives, January 12, 1793.

4. Texas Supreme Court, Paschal vs Pérez, 1851.

5. Chabot, page 116.

6. Buck, *Yanaguana's Successors,* page 31.

7. To reduce confusion about the name associated with their destination, San Antonio de Bejar (Bexar) is the most identifiable. However, it was called Presidio Real de Bexar (Royal Fort of Bexar) and was located on the site of what is now Military Plaza. The original presidio's location in unknown, but the Marques San Miguel de Aguayo chose the site of the presidio that became the nexus of civilization for the Canary Islanders. The village that the Islanders later established around the fort was called Villa de San Fernando de Asurias (Saint Ferdinand of Austria).

8. Read Buck, *Yanaguana's Successors,* for that story.

9. James Michener in his novel *Texas* created a fictional character, Don Ramon de Saldana, who sired seven sons and one daughter. Coincidentally, the fictional character owned a fictional *rancho* on the Medina River.

10. The fortress on the Cibolo, El Fuerte del Cibolo, is

explained in great detail by Robert Thonhoff in his book by that name.

11. Historian and writer Robert Thonhoff describes the first privately owned ranch in Texas as the grant of four leagues and five labors to Andres Hernandez and Luis Menchaca in 1758. *West Texas Historical Association Yearbook,* Volume 40, October 1964.

12. From a document provided by Pérez family descendants.

13. Courbier's earlier interview can be found in the historical section of the San Antonio Public Library. A more lengthy interview followed and is at Appendix A.

14. Andres Tijerina, *Tejanos and Texas Under the Mexican Flag, 1821–1836,* page 9.

15. Frederick Chabot, *With the Makers of San Antonio,* pages 239-240.

16. "Campaign Against the Lipanes," a document written by Andres Benito Courbier in 1798, on file in the San Antonio Public Library.

17. Rosillo Creek begins in NE San Antonio (present-day Windcrest) and runs into Salado Creek south of town. The battle took place on the banks of the Rosillo near its juncture with Salado Creek.

18. *Texas State Historical Association Quarterly,* Volume XI, January 1908, No. 3, *Joaquin de Arredondo's Report of the Battle of the Medina, August 18, 1813,* a translation by Mattie Austin Hatcher, page 230.

19. *The New Handbook of Texas,* Volume 5, page 150.

20. Bexar Archives, 3/12/1814, 053:0562-63, records this as the date Cordero was given permission to marry Gertrudis. An earlier date is given in Carrington, *Women in Early Texas.*

21. Long had pledged his life to establishing a Republic of Texas and wresting the land from Spain. U.S. Secretary of State Henry Clay had claimed Texas was part of the United States by right of the Louisiana Purchase. Usurping the U.S. claim, Long set up a constitutional government in Nacogdoches patterned after the U.S. and began selling land at fifty cents an acre. Both the U.S. and Spain tried to block Long's efforts.

22. This homestead was part of the grant to Joseph Pérez, confirmed in 1777. It was bound on the north by the "parochial church," (San Fernando) on the east by the Acequia Madre, on the south by the street to the creek (Dolorosa), and to the west

by Calle Real (North Flores). The house was situated on the southwest corner of the block.

23. The stone for Gertrudis Peres Cassiano is on the right side of the church behind the altar.

24. In his *1840 Census of the Republic of Texas,* Gifford White lists Jno. Coker, L. Knipp, Lindsey Williams and Agt. A. W. White, James Peacock, and Leal Melchoir, as agents of Ignacio Perez, page 14.

25. The late Charles G. Downing of Eagle Pass, in writing about the history of ranching in that area, was specific about the founding of the Rivas ranch and those who purchased parts of the giant parcel of land.

26. Taken from a county map showing properties along the Medina River, Lee Map Company, Dallas, Texas, circa 1875.

27. A list of those buried within the chapel include Jose Ignacio, who was the first buried in the chapel; Maria Josepha Cortinas Pérez, Jose's wife; Jacob Linn, Jose's son-in-law; Josefa Pérez Linn, Jacob's wife; Ignacio del Refugio Pérez, son of Jose Ignacio; Ignacio Martin Pérez, son of Jose Ignacio; and Trinidad Pérez, daughter of Jose Ignacio.

28. BCA Probate Records, Reel 1019354, #178, 1851–1856, Volume D.

29. Linn's mother died during the voyage and was buried at sea. His father died after their arrival in Texas and was buried at Port Lavaca. His infant sister accompanied him to San Antonio, but died shortly after their arrival.

30. H. Gordon Frost, in his book *I'm Frank Hamer,* does not place Hamer on the ranch, but members of the Walsh family recall his being on the ranch.

31. Telephone conversation with Mrs. Judson Swearingen in Dallas, Texas, January 26, 1999.

32. In 1996, a descendant of the Applewhite family, Herff Applewhite, made headlines as the leader of a California cult called "Heaven's Gate."

33. *San Antonio Express-News,* Sunday, October 12, 1980. Article by Don Walden.

Bibliography

Alonzo, Armando C. *Tejano Legacy, Rancheros and Settlers in South Texas 1734–1900*. Albuquerque, NM: University of New Mexico Press, 1998.

Bernal and others. *A Compact History of Mexico*. El Colegio de Mexico, Mexico 20, DF, 1985.

Bolton, Herbert Eugene. *Bolton and the Spanish Borderlands*. Edited by John Francis Bannon. Norman, OK: University of Oklahoma Press, 1964.

———. *Outpost of Empire*. New York, NY: Alfred A. Knopf, 1931.

———. *Texas in the Middle Eighteenth Century*. Austin, TX: University of Texas Press, 1970 (originally published in 1915 as Volume 3 of The University of California Publications in History).

———. *With the Makers of Texas*. Austin, TX: Gammel–Statesman Publishing Co., 1904.

Buck, Samuel M. *Yanaguana's Successors*, San Antonio, TX: Naylor Company, 1949.

Carrington, Evelyn M. *Women in Early Texas*. Austin, TX: Texas State Historical Association, 1994.

Chabot, Frederick C. *With the Makers of San Antonio*. Privately Published in San Antonio, TX, 1937.

Clayton and Salvant. *Historic Ranches of Texas*. Austin, TX: University of Texas Press, 1993.

Courbier, Andres Benito. *Interview with Y. Pérez*. Historical Document on file in San Antonio Public Library, January 1798.

Daughters of the Republic of Texas Library. Collections and maps at the Alamo, San Antonio, TX.

Fehrenbach, T. R. *Lone Star*. New York: American Legacy Press, 1983.

Frost, H. Gordon. *"I'm Frank Hamer."* Austin, TX: Pemberton Press, 1968.

Habig, Fr. Marion A. O.F.M. *Spanish Texas Pilgrimage.* Chicago, IL: Franciscan Herald Press, 1990.

Hester, Thomas R. *Dipping Into South Texas Prehistory.* San Antonio, TX: Corona Publishing Company, 1980.

Jackson, Jack. *Los Mestenos.* College Station, TX: Texas A&M University Press, 1986.

McGraw, A. Joachim and Kay Hindes. *Chipped Stone and Adobe: A Cultural Resources Assessment of the Proposed Applewhite Reservoir, Bexar County, Texas.* Center for Archaeological Research UTSA, Archaeological Survey Report, No. 163, 1987.

McKellar, Margaret Maud. *Life on a Mexican Ranch.* Edited by Dolores L. Latorre. Cranbury, NJ: Lehigh University Press and Associated University Presses, 1994.

Michener, James A. *Texas.* New York, NY: Random House, 1985.

O'Connor, Kathryn Stoner. *Presidio La Bahia.* Austin, TX: Von Boeckmann–Jones Company, 1966.

Phares, Ross. *The Governors of Texas.* Gretna, LA: Pelican Publishing Company, 1976.

Porter, Lawrence B. *Some Famous Ranches of New Mexico.* Thesis submitted to the New Mexico State University graduate school, Las Cruces, NM, August 1959.

Richardson, Wallace, and Anderson. *Texas: The Lone Star State.* Englewood Cliffs, NJ: Prentice Hall, Inc., 1981.

San Antonio Public Library. Vertical Files, Historical & Genealogy.

Santos, Richard G. *Santa Anna's Campaign Against Texas, 1835-1836.* Second Edition (Revised). Waco, TX: Texian Press, 1968.

Schwarz, Ted. *Forgotten Battlefield of the First Texas Revolution, Battle of Medina.* Edited by Robert Thonhoff. Austin, TX: Eakin Press, 1985.

Spanish and Mexican Land Grants. Arno Press, A New York Times Company, New York, NY, 1974.

Syers, Ed. *Texas: The Beginning 1519-1834,* Waco, TX: Texian Press, 1978.

The New Handbook of Texas. 6 volumes. Austin, TX: Texas State Historical Association, 1996.

Thonhoff, Robert H. *El Fuerte del Cibolo.* Austin, TX: Eakin Press, 1992.

———. *The Texas Connection With the American Revolution.* Austin, TX: Eakin Press, 1981.

Tijerina, Andres. *Tejanos and Texas Under the Mexican Flag, 1821-1836.* College Station, TX: Texas A&M University Press, 1994.

Time-Life Books. *The Spanish West.* New York, NY: Time Inc., 1976.

U.S. Army Corps of Engineers. *Draft Environmental Impact Statement for the Proposed Applewhite Reservoir, Bexar County.* Fort Worth, Texas District, 1987.

Warner, C.A. *Texas Oil and Gas Since 1543.* Houston, TX: Gulf Publishing Company, 1939.

Whisenhunt, Donald W. *Chronology of Texas History.* Austin, TX: Eakin Press, 1982.

White, Gifford. *1840 Census of the Republic of Texas.* Austin, TX: The Pemberton Press, 1966.

Wilkins, Clarice Long. *Applewhite Family.* Genealogy Section, San Antonio Public Library.

Williams, J. W. *Old Texas Trails.* Edited and compiled by Kenneth F. Neighbors, Burnet, TX: Eakin Press, 1979.

Wilson, Maurine T., and Jack Jackson. *Philip Nolan and Texas.* Waco, TX: Texian Press, 1987.

Index